N o Table Too Small

En gaging in the Art and Attitude of Social Change

No Table Too Small by Laura Titzer

Cover Design: Estella Vukovic / estella.vukovic@gmail.com

ISBN: 978-0-692-98548-9

Library of Congress Control Number: 2017908737

Contents

1   Engaging in Change

There is no such thing as a single-issue struggle because we do not live single issue lives.

— Audre Lorde

People are waking to an overwhelming need for change. I can feel it in the pit of my stomach when listening to legislators and news outlets. The status quo has shifted, and extremes are heightening on all sides, creating more extremes, as we all become more polarized in our views and more stuck in our ways.

This societal trend plays out like an argument between two people. One person yells at the other, points a finger, and accuses the other of some offense. Maybe the one offended responds by attacking the accuser's opinions and beliefs. The accuser now goes into defense mode to protect herself. This is done by planting one's feet firmly in her viewpoint, becoming stubborn, and holding on to her view even tighter than before.

This can be observed unfolding between two people, groups of people, and organizations. When it comes to power, the ones who have it don't want to lose it. One can see that when change is happening, they will do whatever is necessary to hold on to their power. This creates polarized extremes. It also creates fear and fear-mongering.

On the edge of change, people are both coming together more and more and are also increasingly separating and fracturing. I see this within the food movement all too often. There are coalitions of nutrition, agriculture, and hunger working together to surpass this edge. At the same time, organizations in this field are pitting themselves against one another and viewing partners as competition. We find ourselves at a precipice of unknowns: unsure of what is really coming and how change could affect all those in the system whether positively or negatively.

We're poised for change either way. Economic, political, social, and environmental forces are so intertwined it is impossible to talk about any one alone. The economic and political forces are a constant action-reaction scenario. This swirls out and affects our social, environmental, and spiritual strata in ways unimaginable and not accounted for by our economists. What ultimately feels important and needed within this divisiveness, fear, and competition is participatory dialogue using the six capabilities of engagement highlighted within this book. From years of working in the food system, I've observed how important these capabilities are for effecting sustainable change. These techniques will help us wade through the murky waters of polarization and bring us together in a space where we are all valued knowledge-holders with unique observations and opinions. The great paradox is that our divisiveness—the reasons certain groups do not get along—are the very things that could give rise to beautiful, integrated social collaboration. A place where we build something totally new together. Based on years of working with change in varying contexts, I've seen the diversity of opinions and backgrounds give rise to this very kind of collaboration. I've seen it work, and I've seen it fail depending on how much a change agent utilized the six capabilities. The pressure of divisiveness offers us a choice: Do we want to let our surroundings fracture us, or do we stay strong and make our bonds even more durable for the challenges ahead? We all know the food system is extremely complex and that we need all kinds of solutions to make it work. It is not a one-size-fits-all from any vantage point.

My intention is to change the way we activate around issues. I envision a movement of all movements coalescing. Where we interact, share, and appreciate each other's talents and leverage these to create a whole new system. For the purpose of this book, "we" refers to activists, advocates, and change agents working at nonprofits, government agencies, community organizations, and for-profits. My voice, and the lens that I write from, is that of a Caucasian female change agent working within nonprofits, and constantly working on being an ally. This makes up my life experience, where I write from, and how I write about it. It is important for anyone conducting change to understand their own purview and where they come from. If you are interested in changing the food system so radically that it is truly representative of everyone in the system, it will be important for others to understand your lens so that they have a more contextual understanding of the experiences that shape your views. Each of us may hold a piece of knowledge on sustainable agriculture, agroecology, industrialized farming, or hunger relief, but we are not experts on these. Your expertise may lie in only one or two areas or generally over all of them. That's why inviting others to the dialogue is essential. By inviting experts in diverse fields, we learn about many different viewpoints. That's the beauty of diversity: I don't have to know everything about everything. I just need to be brave and bold enough to invite others, specifically those I may disagree with, in order to learn from them.

What values and principles do we want the food system to embody? Then, how do we make that a reality? We need to let go of specific, one-size-fits-all solutions and let the values and processes take us where we need to go. Change is a process of becoming which can only be attached to the shared vision and purpose of a diverse and integrated group. Numerous admirable individuals, groups, and organizations do incredible work to change the system. There are many ideas on how to improve the food system: CSA, farmers' markets, community gardens, agroecological methods, to name just a few. We keep telling ourselves that change will happen if we just get more of these things. We are all guilty of this cultural pattern. As a society, Americans tend to be solutions based, not process based. We generally think that *more* of something good will just make the system better. While I like all the above-mentioned activities, we are missing something important. We can't predict the future and the future is always changing. Therefore, it would behoove us to focus more on how we want to get there than what *there* looks like. Our food system has changed immensely over the last one hundred to two hundred years. It doesn't look anything like it once did. The food system is constantly emerging, and full of people who are trying to make it better than it was. We may not always agree on the ways people have attempted to improve the system (or even agree on whether they did in fact improve it), such as with free-trade agreements, genetically modified organisms, industrial-farming practices, or pesticides. However, most, if not all, of these were developed with the intent to make the system more efficient and productive. This in turn would trickle down to make the farmers' life easier and increase food for us all. These were all ideas on how the food system could be improved based on the known scenarios of their times. We don't have to agree with them, and some have had many damaging though unintended consequences. But I think we can all agree that no one invented these things with the core desire to hurt people. Some, such as mechanized-farming practices, were to intentionally make things easier or better. Some, such as confined animal feedlots, were invented to increase profit sharing and organizational growth. Some, like processed foods, were invented to make cooking faster and easier while also working to increase profit sharing.

The food system is deeply interconnected with our economic, environmental, cultural, and political systems. There are strings going every direction to the point where you don't know where one begins and another ends. You're not sure if the food system is affecting another system or if that system is affecting the food system. The truth is that these systems are all affecting each other all the time by creating and reacting to shifts at every moment.

One way of looking at culture is as a system: a broad framework that shapes our behavior and beliefs about how individuals and groups interact. There are many different cultural beliefs and values running parallel, and in some cases opposite, to each other, as well as some cultural beliefs that are held up as the normative ways one should behave above all others. These more dominant cultural beliefs can then exert power and influence over other cultural beliefs and values.

Power follows a loop, beginning with a certain set of cultural beliefs that define the agenda and who gets to participate. This group implements decisions and actions that then loop back around and reinforce the cultural beliefs.

The culture in power, or any culture for that matter, is sustained through stories. The stories we tell ourselves and our friends and family. Culture is also carried on through ancestral stories of myth, gods, mysticism, and magic. Media, and the stories told in television and movies, has played a key role in quickening the pace of change within the food system, for better or worse. However, these stories are fragile, for they depend on constantly renewing and reinforcing the beliefs and desires that legitimize the dominant paradigm. This tends to distribute power unequally as those who are not part of the dominant paradigm — who have different stories — are not included or become marginalized. Because of this inequality in power, those who benefit disproportionally are always engaged in the conscious, and unconscious, maintenance of the current dominant culture. This is something to also be clear on: that the dominant culture is constantly being reinforced unconsciously and consciously. Sometimes, if we are not careful with our words or actions, we can find ourselves guilty of reinforcing the very culture we are trying to challenge.

The effects shape how individuals and groups talk to each other, how we behave and treat each other, how we identify, or do not identify, with other people. It forms our beliefs about what we think we should have or not have; what is right or wrong. Culture also affects what we eat and the types of foods we relate to. I grew up in a Midwest German American household that ate many German dishes and many Midwestern comfort-food dishes. My mother made soups, breads, and sweets from scratch. My grandmother grew all her vegetables and I helped her can green beans. It was mandatory that we ate dinner together. This is a significant part of my food culture and plays a substantial role in what I eat and how I eat to this day. If we are a part of the dominant group, the group for which the system is working well, culture can act as a blinding influence. If the system is working well for them, individuals may not notice the groups for whom the system isn't working. Sidney Rittenburg, who was an American working for the Chinese communist party during the revolution, says in the documentary movie, *The Revolutionary*, that he didn't notice what was wrong because the structure at the time was working for him.[1] He was privileged by it and so was blind to what was happening around him.

Change only happens when people are ready, not necessarily when we think we need it. An important part of getting people ready is highlighting the disconnect between the present state and desired future state. For instance, there is a disconnect between what legislation we want and what is being passed. These disconnects are called inconsistencies. Through repeatedly highlighting these inconsistencies, other people start to see them and get closer to the capacity needed to change. Yes, people only change when they are ready, but we can help nudge them along.

Our political system plays an important role in change. As much as grassroots movements are needed to create new ways of doing things, it is critical for grassroots efforts to affect policies within the food system. Activists can't merely keep working and hope that one day large corporations will eventually follow our lead. They must be included and held accountable in the process to create sustained and integrated change. If a healthy food system is the desired outcome, policies need to be in place that protect and promote such a system.

The best and only place to begin is where we're at: getting individuals to feel *powerful* instead of *powerless*. One reason I like President Obama is because of his community-organizing background, which shone through every now and then in his presidency. In many of his speeches he called the people to action; that if we want to see change, we need to raise our voices and call our legislators. Remember that our legislators represent us; they do not dictate rules to us. A few days after one of President Obama's declarations to the people of the United States, Jon Stewart criticized him for, in so many words, deflecting the problem to us. Stewart continued to say that he's the president so it's his job. As soon as President Obama tried to rally people to act, he was criticized and individuals were reminded by a widely watched television-show host that we shouldn't be acting. This takes our power.

Our environmental system interacts a bit differently than the others. It aligns itself to rules we only slightly understand. We communicate with the environment in the ways that we treat the water, soil, and air. In turn, the world communicates back with reactions and responses, such as the dead zones in the Gulf of Mexico, quickly melting ice caps, dried-up soils, or beautiful loam, bountiful crops, and healthy animals. We do have ideas on how to treat the planet so that it is here for future generations. These may include limiting pesticide and antibiotic use or growing in a more diverse and sustainable way. A forest will have layer upon layer of plant life beginning with the forest floor and moving all the way up to the tallest trees. Each layer has different insects, animals, and plant life inhabiting it. These layers and their patterns are replicable throughout an entire forest down to the shape of a leaf. Change agents can easily take this natural order of diversity as an important model for our own lives.

The economic system, much like the political, is inextricably linked to culture. The political affects the economic structure and vice versa, while the cultural system affects and is affected by both the aforementioned. The current economic system did not come into being overnight and provides a powerful example of how social change is a marathon. Gain for gain's sake was criminal up until the mid- to late 1600s because the culture at the time was innately opposed to such an idea.[2] The profit motive present today was considered a sin. Many change agents worked tirelessly to change this and at the time were considered outcasts. These outcasts worked on many different political and educational levels with a relentless passion to see what they believed were better ways to come to fruition. At the end of the day, many of us also believe in a better way, a better food system. Having a vision for something better is what makes many of us change agents.

Most of the economic scholars for the past hundred or more years have told us that growth is good, to the point where this has solidified in our culture as truth. It's always more whether talking of money, number of people served, or number of pounds distributed. The only way that happens is by expansion of products, services, or programs. However, there are other ways of calculating growth or success for a company and many are doing just this. Even over the last fifteen years, books have been published about values-driven companies that are getting away from this growth model. Yet, this isn't mainstream. Capitalists faced an institutionalized system when attempting to change the structure hundreds of years ago. Most people at that time thought the current system worked and that the new ideas of Capitalism were ludicrous or even criminal. These new economic change agents believed there was a better way of doing business whether or not you agree with the outcome. These individuals stuck by what they believed in and took relentless incremental steps toward their larger vision. They remained patient and worked on the system through education and making changes when and where they were able. This was a change that shifted our entire way of doing business. If any of us want to completely overhaul the food system, we need to harness aspects of these determined change agents. There are important lessons here that we can use, while also remembering that such massive change takes time.

The environmental, cultural, political and economic systems, when viewed together, show us our current position. The food system is inextricably woven into all of them. It is important to know how any social change work being done affects these systems and how people on all sides of us, whether for or against change, are crucial to keep in the fold.

How do we encourage change and support its process? This is an important question, as many of us dislike change in our day-to-day life. We struggle with change even though we know it is inevitable. That is why this work is so difficult yet important. The process of change is an ongoing paradox of knowing that it is constant yet not wanting things to change. If we are so resistant to change in our personal lives, then change in any other way is going to be just as difficult. We like things to stay the same even when the status quo isn't working because we feel that it is better to know than to change to something that is unknown. We tend to get stuck in this thinking that knowing is better than not knowing. This isn't the case, if for nothing else than what we think we know is an illusion.

According to Julie Battilana and Casciaro Tiziana, who wrote an article in the Harvard Business Review, "Change is hard, especially in a large organization. Numerous studies have shown that employees tend instinctively to oppose change initiatives because they disrupt established power structures and ways of getting things done."[3] As mentioned earlier, power plays an important role in change. Established power is threatened by change. Those ruled by this established power may also feel fear over a new structure. The idea of the change agent has popped up in healthcare, education, social work, business, and activism. The reason it has surfaced across so many sectors is because of our inherent stigma against change. The greatest paradox might indeed be that we are surrounded by constant change yet we can't stand it to the point that we basically run screaming in the opposite direction. Of course, the other paradox is that we want everyone else to change in line with our own ideas and for our own self to stay the same.

Do we turn our backs on certain ideas because we strive to be different than entities that we view as enemies? It is only our loss if we do. All the people, groups and organizations that are in our food system currently cannot simply be ignored or pushed out. We have to accept that we are here. It doesn't mean we must agree with each other. But we must recognize where we are currently as objectively as possible. We are not the only ones willing to change, or the only ones thinking we have the solutions to save our food system. Ideas are coming in from all directions and there isn't just one silver-bullet idea out there for our complex system. Change requires that we include opposing opinions by finding a common spark while retaining the ability to function.

If change is always constant, why does it seem that people refuse to change their minds on an issue and instead dig their feet in? It is because our paradigms become much more rigid, especially when it feels like everything is changing around us. Social change theorist John Dewey speaks of ways paradigms can change in his theory of experiential learning.[4] Dewey suggests we consider learning as a developmental spiral where the learning from one cycle stimulates the beginning of another and so on, thereby providing us with a process that allows us to reconstruct our knowledge and skills in light of new experiences. Constant change meets social change. The answer to why people refuse to change their minds is that if we aren't working toward shifting paradigms with dynamic and diverse learning experiences, then people will dig in their feet and continue to hold on to what they know to be true. John Dewey's model flows like this: We move along in our current experience happily until there is a disturbance. From here, we begin reflecting with others on this disturbance and amplifying actions of change. Next, we begin to self-organize and create alternatives. We can be at this stage for a while because this stage is ultimately trying to create new understanding and paradigms to solidify change. The cycle ends with a new experience and paradigm. Then, once again, we remain here happily until another disturbance. The process continually goes on in cycles just like this.

Let's dig in a bit deeper here. At the beginning of any change, we each have a set of beliefs and models that inform the way we see the world and understand experiences. For example, let's use two camps of people. Those who solely believe in industrial, corporate agribusiness and those who solely believe in local, small and sustainable agriculture. The two groups apply their current paradigms to the at-hand experiences. If a desired outcome is achieved that fits within their current paradigm, they rinse and repeat. This cycle typically requires little self-reflection, because things are going well. It's like being on autopilot. However, what happens if the intended outcome is not achieved or there appears to be a disturbance? Let's say you're walking along, gliding down a sidewalk, and then, suddenly, you trip and fall. Typically, we might stand up, look around for what we may have tripped on — along with looking embarrassed — and then continue walking with potentially a little more attention. A similar disturbance can happen during a project, program, or movement where suddenly something trips and we find ourselves actually noticing the ground and our feet. For instance, the agribusiness or local agriculture paradigms may find disturbances if they come across information that speaks against their beliefs. We may feel surprised, confused or unsure of what is happening or going wrong. We will not look for fixes that go against our paradigms in a closed loop. However, if we add a loop to learn from others' experiences and allow ourselves to be challenged in a safe environment, we may find a solution to the disturbance that creates systemic change through experiential learning. In social change, a disturbance provides a pivotal moment for intervention. The role of the change agent is to leverage these disturbances and create learning moments that strive to shift paradigms. These would be called "moments of intervention." Ways in which we can intervene include facilitated conversations, protests, rebellions, and even laws, taxes, and policies. Facilitated conversations with diverse groups provide the space to evolve, emerge, and self-organize into new systems providing space to experiment with alternatives and create paradigm shifts. Facilitated conversations also open the flow of information between varying groups creating cross-pollination. A quick note: when I speak of a paradigm shift using agribusiness and small agriculture as an example, I'm not inferring that these two groups need to duel out their paradigms until there is only one standing. A paradigm shift can be to something completely new. Later in the book we will talk more about how to get to shared visions that can create new paradigms.

The most influential point of change is paradigms. For change to become a new steady state (until the next iteration), we must shift our underlying assumptions and ways of being. Something to remember now and throughout this book is that individuals are not resisting change; rather they are simply holding on to what they know to be true, which affects their capacity to change. We must find ways, as I'll point out later, to bring these individuals along with us. Managing these different stages of readiness and ability for change is the scaffolding that supports the system during the tenuous period. Without proper investment in the infrastructure to make something work, the system simply cannot support the demands. It is like getting the land for a farm, but missing the seeds. Or having the seeds but nowhere to plant, or lacking all the needed tools to properly harvest, sow, and maintain the plants. In the food system, we need to make sure we create the capacity for the change we want to see, so that the change can be sustained. For instance, enough people must support the change for it to be sustainable, along with policies to help promote and support the change. We must also be able to see how we relate to others' viewpoints in a safe way so that we can actually take in alternative perspectives and begin to learn from others and understand their experiences. This builds our personal capacity for change and begins the process of paradigm shifting and shared visions. Lastly, we must be able to reflect in action by seeing what is happening in the moment and responding to it accordingly even if it means throwing out something of your own.

Now that a foundation for engaging with change has been provided, it is time to dive into the process by which we may be able to change the food system. When we talk about a process for engaging our food system, it is not a simple three- or five-step manual. It is an interconnected and converging guide that helps direct us when confronting varying situations. The toughest part about all this work, about everything in this book, is how we must work together. It is the toughest and the most important. How can we have a diverse, functioning, healthy system? Engagement, patience, and humility (non-ego). We need patience as we work through our current individualistic and polarized groups to become more integrated and collaborative. We need patience as we work through the entrenched negativity and divisive language habits that we've formed. Checking our ego at the door is also critical. What I think or what my organization does are not the bees' knees of social change, nor does it need to be the leader in that change. Needing to be recognized as an owner of a change activity usually ends up trumping the change you set forth to accomplish, mainly because that means the change is being controlled by the person wanting the recognition, and that means that the change is not communal, social, and built together.

Engagement is the committing of time and energy to set something in motion. It is sharing in an activity or producing a reaction. There are certain capabilities that aid in engaging others in any work. Each of us should constantly work at improving ourselves in these areas, moving from a novice to an expert, knowing all the while that to be an expert means that one never stops learning. There are six capabilities that are the most important when engaging with others to create change. In the following chapters I will discuss these six and what it takes to cultivate engagement in ourselves and others.

Keep these questions in mind as you think about your own steps in change.

1. What is your intention?
2. What are the potential positive and negative consequences of the change you seek?
3. How do you incorporate, leverage, and appreciate different views and opinions to create change?
4. Who's missing from the conversation that can create diverse views?
5. How do you deal with conflict and paradox?
6. What assumptions do you need to test?
7. What conversation, if begun today, could ripple out in a way that creates new possibilities for the future?
8. What unique contribution can you make?

2   Capability One: Holding Space

When we hold the space for someone we are just present, listening, and validating. We aren't judging, giving advice or offering a solution. It is not difficult to hold space, just remember this easy rule, if you hold the space, you'll create the place. Intention is the key.

— *Rea Curry*

One could wrap this entire book with the word "engagement." How we engage with people or groups we disagree with and how we engage with our allies will make or break the movement. In coalitions that I've watched falter, it is how we come to the table, how we've decided to engage, that directs it. If ego comes to the table, then egos will prevail and no such collaboration will continue. Engagement, how we take that first step, and how we choose to interact, sets the stage. It sets the agenda and setting the agenda controls who isn't there and what isn't discussed.

The process of engagement is found in how we hold space. It's the container in which the meeting, group, or coalition convenes. This includes our intentions and assumptions that we bring when we arrive and the setting in which we meet. If we assume that a participant will be difficult or not understanding, then that will affect how we engage. If our intention is to prove someone wrong or prove ourselves right, this of course also affects not only how we engage, but how the others will engage or not. Holding space requires facilitating a room to bring benefit to others and to empower participants to develop their potential while leaving space for others to contribute. This means that the agenda should be created by all showing up, especially with something as complex as our food system. To provide a space where people feel included and empowered, their concerns must be included whether we agree with them or not. Ultimately, holding space means creating a space in which differing opinions can exist. We need to remember that different viewpoints do not have to equal conflict. With that, holding space involves ensuring a safe place for people to communicate, to answer difficult questions, and to explore tough subjects and emotions. Lastly, expertly holding space allows for the emergence of the unexpected, which means we need to be ready to work with ambiguity.

I facilitate with the sole purpose of moving groups to a shared vision, purpose, and action plan. When I looked at the first workshop we were to hold for a farm-to-food pantry meeting, at first blush it seemed that the only people who needed to be there were food banks and growers. However, I questioned immediately who else should be there if I let go of my assumptions. In so doing, we invited health professionals, extension agents, farmers' market managers among many others. I and my staff told each of these groups to invite anyone else who they thought might be interested. Who knew where pivotal relationships would come from? Additionally, I knew that the more diverse group we had, the more interesting the conversation could be. It helps people get unstuck from their particular professional silo. So, our intention from the beginning was to set aside any assumptions and to be as inclusive as possible.

Next, came the space. These workshops are held in communities in which I do not live. I wanted the setting to be reflective of the conversation and comfortable for the participants. We had monetary constraints, so it's not as if we could have the meetings anywhere, but they needed to be given consideration. We worked with our community contacts on what would be the most ideal meeting place. Some of our meetings have been where the farmers' market is held, a grange hall, or a community action center. But it doesn't end here. Now we had to think about how the room was laid out. What would provide the best promotion of communication and sharing of ideas? Basically, the flow of the agenda needs to guide the set-up of the space to maximize this. Building agendas quite possibly take the most time and should for good reason. While they are completely laid out with up to four pages with intense detail, they still had to allow for emergence of what may happen in the moment. You may be wondering how to craft an agenda that provides space for the unknown. It's not as hard as it sounds if you're letting the group build the discussion and trust that whatever the outcome is what the group built together. This means that the agenda must be built by the group and have time for discussion and planning. I've seen the difference between building an agenda without the community and with the community. The difference can be amazing.

In the former, we believed we were building an agenda that mattered to the participants. The topics we built in were based on months of conference and one-on-one calls. We knew what they needed more information on. Our first assumption. We had a great idea on how to help move the communities forward. On the day of one specific workshop, we began with some presentations on a few topics and then I dived into the main discussion. I presented what we were going to work on for the remainder of the time. I had thought long and hard about the right questions. I had maps, markers, and paper. I was excited. I posed my question. Crickets. I retraced some steps and posed the question differently. Deadly silence and eyes staring at me almost blankly. Here's where allowing for emergence and refraining from getting stuck to the agenda is handy. Instead of continuing to push the conversation, I stopped and said "Okay, let's try this a different way." I put down the agenda and asked them what issues they would like to tackle. We ended up having a fruitful conversation because it was one that they built. I learned a lot about my assumptions that day.

In the latter workshop example, we held multiple meetings with community members about what the agenda should look like. I built a suggested-agenda outline and then they added and filled in what they said would matter to their community. The workshop was night and day compared to the previous. It flowed. There were intense conversations where people were making new connections and creating new initiatives. In these examples, it matters little what I get out of it as I'm doing this solely for the community that I'm in. I am holding space and providing a container to develop connections and ideas. However, even if I held one of these in my own community it wouldn't change the approach. If you are trying to create forward movement you must create an inclusive container.

With that being said, we must get the whole system in the room. This might not seem earth-shattering, but when this idea was first discussed among social theorists, it heralded a revolution in democratic participation within organizations because it pulled departments together that typically didn't communicate. Here, we can easily insert system instead of organization. If we think of our food system like an organization that is large, a little unruly, and containing multiple departments that don't get along, then we start to get an idea of who should be in the room. Many different communities need to be there, which means we're probably going to need a pretty large room. I've attended many a summit where it is featured that the whole system is in the room: health, nutrition, farm, hunger-relief, etc. are all there. There are immigrants, people of color, and tribal representation. But is this everyone in the system or is it merely everyone in the system whom we want to talk with? This kind of summit is having a whole system in the room of only mutually agreeing people while keeping potential opponents at bay. It is hardly getting the actual whole system in the room. This is a closed-loop conversation where we all sit around and nod in agreement with each other and pat one another on the back for a job well done and find new ways to collaborate within this closed loop. At some of the workshops I've held, we've had naysayers present. Sometimes it was difficult to manage the differing opinions, but they end up always adding something worth keeping in mind within the project at hand. It's always important to keep in mind who isn't present.

We talk about the other side, our opponents, as if we know them like the back of hand without ever actually inviting to directly hear from them. We are not challenging our assumptions, only ingraining them deeper in this process. It's like any time you are drawn into a discussion where another, who becomes the other, is talked about with gross assumptions being made about her the entire time. The other never gets a chance to speak because she wasn't there. The individuals present, because of this, get to continue making and believing their stories. Instead, we can get excited to be around people who may think very different from us. It can be interesting and exciting to learn how others might view the same problem if we come with that intention to allow ourselves to learn from others. That would be a powerful summit.

I was recently at a talk that highlighted some fears that activists may have of inviting such opponents to the table. The opponents will lie. They will say whatever they want because they don't care. While it has been proven in some cases that a corporation has lied, so has it been proven that many individuals have lied. The next statement is made in no way to diminish any lack of trust an organization or corporation has created. What if those lies are to protect their organization or corporation so that it remains thriving? Depending on your job position, a main goal one has is to keep the company floating above water and seen positively by the public. Or at the very least, to maintain the stability of your own job. It may be a defense mechanism that we need to find a way around. As was said earlier, there are trust issues between the varying groups within the food system that we will have to contend with when doing this kind of change work. It doesn't mean that we should suddenly believe blindly what one might be telling us, but we will have to suspend our assumptions that someone might always be lying. This fear and belief builds a wall between us that will prevent sustainable change work from ever truly happening. This will in turn prevent any whole-system change from taking place. Someone has to extend the olive branch first and be willing to suspend judgments for a moment to begin breaking down the wall.

A position within an organization or system can define that person, her outlooks and interests, making her a prisoner of the group's identity. This can work positively by providing us places to connect with like-minded people and help us feel connected. It can also negatively affect us by constraining our beliefs, assumptions, and actions. What to do when we are faced with being constrained by the groups we belong to? I have felt this constraint or expectation to fall into the group stereotypes. When I fall out of these definitions people get defensive or confused as if by not being exactly like the stereotype it calls into question the whole group. If we are constrained by our actions within a group, all the more reason that we must change the group, as well as the individual self. This kind of group think that happens binds us and prevents us from learning, growing, and being open-minded. On the other side, if we are targeting someone within another group and asking the person to change, we may not have any luck. Maybe we feel that the person is lying, growing defensive, and simply not listening to us. Think about it, we are asking someone to stand out from the group she belongs to which can sound, and be, terrifying. For the same reasons we identify and feel safe within our groups, others feel safe within theirs and will not be easily persuaded otherwise.

Defined groups and their identities tend to divide the world into "them" and "us" based on a process of social categorization. If our self-esteem is to be maintained our group needs to compare favorably with other groups. This is critical to understanding prejudice, because once two groups identify themselves as rivals they are forced to compete for the members to maintain their beliefs and assumptions. Competition and hostility between groups is thus not only a matter of competing for resources, but also the result of competing identities and the protection of them. This takes us a step deeper into group identity and starts to explain why groups naturally tend to be pitted against each other. Think about it. What if you spent your whole life believing that grass was green only to find that one day it turns out that grass is yellow? The green-grass group had staked their identities for a long time based on grass being green. To learn one day that this isn't so is a forced paradigm shift and would take some time for that group to fully grasp the new information. It deconstructs their group identity. The group becomes at risk of losing itself; who it understands itself to be. Not only that the individuals in the group must reassess their beliefs and assumptions if the identity was so closely aligned to grass being green. This is a simplistic example, but provides insight into varying beliefs that we carry about the food system. Calling someone wrong and yourself right, even including facts and figures, may not be what it takes to work together.

Activists and advocates must realize that the seemingly simplistic nature of convincing someone of your viewpoint is not about right and wrong. It's not about who has the best facts and research. It's about protecting identities and world views. What kind of creative sparks could arise if our group walls softened and people from other groups were allowed in? This requires us to loosen our grip on how we see ourselves and the groups we belong to. We will need to move from an either/or to a both/and frame of mind and identity. As F. Scott Fitzgerald stated, "The test of a first-rate intelligence is the ability to hold two opposed ideas in mind at the same time and still retain the ability to function."[5]

These two concepts challenge us to think about who are all the stakeholders in our food system. A stakeholder is a person or group that has an investment, share, or interest in something, as a business or industry. Obviously, when discussing the food system that means everyone is a stakeholder. This makes the work of changing the food system complex and messy. We are all different. We were each raised differently, have a different relation to food, were schooled in a myriad of ways and have a multitude of ways of solving problems within the food system. So, in no way does looking at things systemically make moving forward easier. It does make changing the food system more holistic, honest, and inclusionary toward all. For example, at my place of employment I work with many different staff on the programs I manage. My process for each program has been the same: get all the staff who touch the project in any way in the same room to review the program. It makes for a lot of people in the room. In these meetings, I ask what isn't working and then ask whoever speaks up what she would do to fix it. From there, we find a fix that makes sense for everyone. This process creates buy-in and responsibility within the group. I've watched it work time and again. I don't pretend to know others' jobs and I do expect them to know theirs and take responsibility for it.

Sometimes people get irritated at the meetings and wonder why they should come. I have received the feedback time and again that these same individuals who might get tired of my constant invite feel appreciative and involved in the project. The people who were frustrated now help me to accomplish projects and problem-solve because I engage with them at all levels and ask them for their solutions. On one hand, this inclusionary and systemic process does create some ease in the process because all involved have buy-in and are actively working on their pieces, which also tends to make them more engaged and willing to help when there is a crisis. It creates ease for me personally because I'm not trying to come up with all the answers. The answers come from each person in the group. This is how I create recommendations in making programs better. On the other hand, this process is also arduous and at times exhausting. It can make for more work, and at times I feel exhausted or wonder if what I'm doing is working. I don't have this feeling just with internal meetings but also with the workshops I facilitate. Constantly trying to be as inclusionary as possible is hard work. Even more, facilitating that group can be just as tiresome. Being completely inclusionary takes intention, mindfulness, patience, self-care, and self-awareness. At the end of the day, I've seen this process of complete inclusion create highly effective groups that have a collective impact within integrated collaboration. In a third round of workshops in one community, when I was particularly feeling this way, a woman came up to me at the very beginning and said that she was very thankful of the time we've spent holding these workshops and that without them none of the work they've accomplished would have happened. She went on to say that simply creating a space where people could collaborate and empower themselves was what they needed and that was what I provided. This feedback also helped me see the intention we needed to carry in future workshops in other communities. This example provides fodder as to our need to cross boundaries that we have typically refrained from crossing and being inclusive of all stakeholders, not just the ones who share our same ideas. Where in the food system might we share values, but differ in solutions and implementation?

In my work, I strive to bring all stakeholders to the meetings. Continuous engagement, even if someone may not like you, eventually breaks down those walls and suddenly it gets easier. There is much less pushback. Instead they provide their own ideas and might say "Sure, that sounds easy enough." I leave the room feeling like some miracle just happened. It wasn't a miracle; it was the work of engaging all the people who need to be there. In fact, I've been in circumstances where I've been told that some individuals are just difficult and I should just leave them out of the conversation. Every time I'm told this, those difficult people get immediately added to my invite list. For those are the people I need at the table. It's called managing polarities. The ones that feel the furthest away are the ones who we need to tend to the most. If for nothing else than those difficult people will continue to make things difficult until they are engaged. Once they are engaged consistently it's hard for them to keep up the difficult behavior because people are now paying attention to them. It's easy to complain when you don't feel like you are being included. But once you are being actively included it gets harder and harder to complain. The person who is initiating that engagement is removing those barriers and putting the onus on that seemingly difficult person. Most people are only being difficult for the very reason of not feeling engaged in the dialogue. This is about facilitating those dialogues and bringing people together in a way that creates greater flows of information and transforming exchanges. It is a way of convening that demands emergence, engagement, and active participation. It requires individuals to be actors and not simply observers.

How do we deal with such potential polarities? The motivation for change must be generated before the actual change can occur. To prove this idea of motivation, Kurt Lewin, a social psychologist, conducted a study during World War II aimed at persuading American housewives to buy cheaper cuts of meat.[6] He concluded that it is much easier to change someone's mind by supplying all the information and letting her decide through group discussion than it is dictating to her how to change. This, along with other studies, confirmed that a participatory process of change was far superior to an expert-centered approach. What does this mean? We can't yell and dictate to the individuals we view as opponents what we think they should do. To raise the tipping point and start motivating people to change, we need to have conversations that include even those we gravely disagree with about the issues. Discussing all sides, not just what we think is right, so that a truly systemic conversation is cocreated where people come to a collective decision about what should be done. Otherwise, we are guilty of the expert-driven approach by simply telling people who we are trying to change what should be done and expecting them to follow. Individuals and businesses on both sides of change are guilty of this. The ones we are trying to convince with our expertise, have their own expertise that they try to push onto us. Next thing you know we are in a scrimmage, shoulder to shoulder, both sides pushing as hard as they can. What happens? Nothing.

What happens if we provide a space where information from all sides is presented and discussed? It's limitless really. New ideas, solutions, partnerships, and visions abound. This is where change begins again and again. I'm sure someone is thinking right now, "Yeah, we've tried that, and it doesn't work; no one listens to the other side." Indeed, because both parties think that they are right and the other is wrong meaning that neither party thinks they can learn from the other.

What Lewin's example shows is that through facilitated group discussions we can provide a space where change — or the motivation for change — can begin to take shape. There are many ways to facilitate small groups and in my experience, if performed with intentional questions and the space for open and diverse views, can be quite transformative and a primary source of learning. I can attest to this personally. The workshops and meetings that I have facilitated, no matter the purpose, have only been successful when a group is brought together that represents different parts of the system. In these scenarios, the group learns from each other and when this happens the people who are ready for change help to motivate others who aren't quite there yet as they are pulled into possibilities that begin to feel safe. These possibilities begin to feel safe because the group is discussing them together, adding their concerns, their views, challenges, and successes. In the workshops mentioned earlier, the ones that were unsuccessful had a top-down approach.

Even though I was supplying space for conversation, I was forcing what the conversation should be. For individuals or groups to feel willing to change, they must have a voice in what the conversations will be about. It must be participatory. The facilitator is holding space and creating the container, not dictating the discussion.

Our conflict-averse nature has created a space where difference of opinion among a group is not wanted and even seen as conflicting and negative, but it is this very thing we want and need to solve problems big and small. This is the type of diverse group work we need to change the food system. It is precisely this diligent group work that digs into collaborating with collective impact and real social change. As has been stated, this type of work will be difficult and asks us to do some uncomfortable things that we have been told not to do. This type of collaboration asks us to be bold and strong so that we can suspend our preconceived assumptions. If we cannot suspend these even for a few moments while being open to generative learning and listening, this work will not succeed.

Tension and conflict are often created through new, or differing, ideas clashing with existing ones. We end up in conflict because of our values, which are core to our identity, or our interests, perceptions, or the way something is communicated. The depth of the conflict depends on which one of these it's hitting up against. Perception or the way something is communicated is surface-level conflict. Conflict over values and interests gets into deeper conflict as patterns, experiences, and relationships come into play. It will help if we begin to look at different opinions, no matter how different, not as potential conflict, but as potential learning. Develop a personal capacity that embraces conflicting approaches while retaining the ability to function. Maybe we need to replace the word "conflict" altogether with what it is: different views. This isn't to say that a conflict won't arise in these situations as they surely might. Some researchers believe that achieving resolution through synthesizing ideas into one will only prevent future change and can be less productive than creating a space where the opposing ideas work in tandem. This dives deeper into why diversity of views and opinions is so important. Group think only creates an environment where a complex, changing system cannot exist. It suffocates the system causing it to become unhealthy and stagnant. Think about monocropping. While this is good for large machinery and is certainly one way of farming, it also leaves out all diversity. Soil suffers, superweeds form, and even some superbugs. Lack of diversity suffocates the system and creates even more problems. We can't just have one way of modeling the food system or it will become unhealthy. It needs to be open to numerous ways of sustaining our system that appreciates that there might need to be agroecology methods, small farms, large farms, industrialized farms, and so many others.

As a change agent attempting to hold space and sit in this fluid state of emergence, understanding diversity becomes tantamount. Diversity is a spectrum of views, opinions, experiences, and cultures. Diversity also requires us to have skills in cultural competency. Okokon O. Udo, a professor of Integrative Health and Wellness at Northwestern Health Sciences University, has said that "To be culturally competent doesn't mean that you are an authority in the values and beliefs of every culture. What it means is that you hold a deep respect for cultural differences and are eager to learn, and willing to accept, that there are many ways of viewing the world." [7] This elicits a broader thought behind cultural competency than the most obvious. At first glance, one might readily say cultural competency is important when interacting with different cultures. This is correct thinking, but there is something more to this phrase. We are all distinctly different from someone else based on where we grew up, how we grew up, gender identity, or race. There are also the aspects of age, ability, education, religion, political views, socio-economic status, and so on.

I sat in on a cultural competency workshop where the presenter was African American and was telling a story about how she thought she could identify with other African American women. She soon found out that even within that grouping there were differences to be bridged. I have felt this within groups that I identify with as well. That assumption that we are all the same because we identify with a certain group only to find out that there are great differences within. This is cultural competency: realizing that we are all different even within the groups we identify. In another workshop on cultural competency, we were asked to pair up and answer a series of questions. The answers were basic, but very revealing of different life paths. Even more, this highlighted that our unique life experiences caused each of us to perceive and respond to situations differently.

There are steps we can take to be more culturally competent, such as having an awareness of self and others. When in conversation, we can acknowledge what the other is saying in a sincere form. Genuinely validating what the other has just stated is another step. This operates from a place of knowing that whatever one feels as her truth cannot be wrong. It can't be wrong because it is a felt emotion or opinion. I may not agree with it because my truths are different. Just as you feel your opinions are right and true, so does another. Neither of us are wrong or right. It is not about that. It is about having different opinions and feelings on subject matters, seeing this conflict and being able to work through it. Conflict typically arises here in the difference of opinion or of our cultural milieu. Conflict arises from assuming that someone is like us, or demonizing her based on where she works or groups she is associated with, or in managing polarities or different starting points within change. Conflict is inherent because we are all different and at different ready points within social change. We have various ways of solving the same issues. Ultimately, conflict is natural because paradoxes are naturally occurring.

There is no conflict resolution, only conflict management, which leads us to the last step in cultural competency, negotiation. Once we both have our truths out in the open and each of us has been acknowledged and validated, we can then move into the action of how we will move forward. But how do we negotiate if we have differing opinions where we each think that ours is the "right" one? It is not easy, and only one of you may be interested in negotiation. In some instances, neither party may be interested in negotiation. Not every scenario will have both parties eager to hear out the other. I challenge you to be the person who wants to acknowledge the other and move into sincere negotiation.

To move forward and beyond from our differing opinions, we must shift from the position to the issue. The position is one's opinion on the matter, which is of course that individual's truth. What needs to happen when acting as facilitator and holding space, is to identify the issues behind the position. We also need to identify the values we carry. What I mean here is that we need to find out why we each care about the issue and what makes us care about it to even have an opinion. This is where we get to our intention; what brought us to the meeting in the first place. It's where the meat is and where we can begin to negotiate working together.

The reason this is so important to the task at hand — changing the food system — is because we must learn the skill of cultural competency to work with others to effect any real change. Cultural competency asks us to embrace diversity within opinions, paradigms, beliefs, cultures, ethnicities, orientations, desires, and truths within the system. There are many ways to build a food system and currently we are all fighting tooth and nail to be the one that rises to the top. For all the clamor of agroecology, which at its core is about increased diversity, many individuals paradoxically shut down to the thought of diverse opinions of the food system. Without a genuine approach to diversity, without the strength to have one's own opinions challenged and broadened, we all risk never creating change over the long term, but only moments in time where something different bubbled up and then dissipated. To the risk of our ego, we need to relinquish it by realizing that we can have our opinions and learn from others. Without cultural competency, how will we ever pull the ones not ready for change into our sphere when holding space? How will we emerge leaders if we are not fostering differing opinions? The expert-driven culture runs deep in the United States and prevents us from developing our competence and understanding toward others with different views.

When we find ourselves in scenarios where we are the conveners and facilitators, how we hold the space is the first and crucial step. We need to think about the whole system bringing in as many diverse viewpoints as possible so that we can have rich, learning dialogues. We must create an environment that is safe for participants to share their views. Sometimes this takes the form of creating group norms at the beginning or having each person state her intentions or even both. It requires building an agenda with the group. You can have a foundation-level agenda, but there must be room to add in topics that the group members care about. As an example, something I've done in the past is after stating why we were brought together and what the plan of the meeting looks like, I then ask if anyone wants to add anything. If there are many suggestions, we group them into categories. All of this is encapsulated by the need to be cognizant of conflict and managing differing viewpoints by creating a space with inclusive and participatory group discussions.

Releasing the Need for Results

To clarify this concept further, here is a letter to a friend from Thomas Merton: "Do not depend on the hope of results...you may have to face the fact that your work will be apparently worthless and even achieve no result at all, if not perhaps results opposite to what you expect. As you get used to this idea, you start more and more to concentrate not on the results, but on the value, the rightness, the truth of the work itself...You gradually struggle less and less for an idea and more and more for a specific people...In the end, it is the reality of personal relationship that saves everything." [8]

In creating our interconnectedness, we must become flexible to the results we envision. Everyone has a slightly different result she may want to see. In my group work, I relinquish any desire toward a specific result. I put the weight on the process because I know if the process is well thought out and well facilitated, the results will be exactly what they need to be. This happens because there is a form of integrative collaboration taking place, there is high inclusion, and silo thinking is being bridged among different groups of people. In these group processes we access the shared values among the team and move forward from that space.

3   Capability Two: Communication

To effectively communicate, we must realize that we are all different in the way we perceive the world and use this understanding as a guide to our communication with others.

— *Tony Robbins*

Ideas are given meaning through their connections, the actions taken on them, and their translations. Interpretation occurs when the idea is connected to already understood words and values. This is not unlike strategic messaging. The values associated with a certain idea will dictate its translation. This in turn helps one decide if an action is taken or not. If the values that are portrayed by that idea are a value I hold then I'm taken to positive action. If, however, the values are not what I hold then I might be taken to negative action. Think about words like "industrial farming," "sustainable," "organic," "monocrop" and the weight they hold and the values they insinuate. How we get others to connect to our ideas depends on how we talk about them. Are we connecting to only what we care about or are we connecting to what someone else might care about? For instance, how would one connect industrial farming to someone who opposes it or discuss agroecology with someone who is pro-industrial farming? How do we look at those words, and the values behind them, to find linkages that could possibly connect us?

There are four key parts of communication that show up throughout this chapter: deep listening, asking questions, relating to others, and empathy. Deep listening requires listening for the energy and emotion as well as the words. It's the act of understanding, interpreting, and evaluating what you hear with intuitive openness. The skill of asking questions demands that we ask powerful questions that will make a difference, engage people, and focus the attention on the choices. It's the craft of asking questions that strengthen a system's capacity to apprehend, anticipate, and heighten positive potential. Asking questions inherently demands us to leave our assumptions at the door. Relating well to others means that we need to relate to and collaborate with people from different, as well as the same, cultural, professional, and institutional contexts. At an intermediate level, relating with others is recognizing and responding to mental models from a variety of backgrounds while listening actively with empathy. At an expert level, it is possessing the skill to challenge and shift mental models while understanding and responding to a variety of cultures, experiences, and backgrounds and understanding the intricacies in seemingly similar cultural contexts. Empathy asks us to have the ability to connect with another person from within by placing yourself in that person's position and seeing the world through her eyes.

Communication is all these things wrapped into finding common ground, managing polarities, and learning how to address the issues and the people in different ways that promotes change. We need to think about the words we use when speaking to people's feelings, have an awareness of communication strategies, and the ability to leverage them based on the needs of the situation.

We will be in discussion with people we may not readily get along with. In these scenarios, we must search for common ground. A few years ago, a conference I attended had a theme around building just this. There was one transformative discussion that took place Saturday morning. Lawrence Lessig, a Harvard Law professor and campaign finance-reform activist, and Tea Party Patriots cofounder Mark Meckler discussed building left-right alliances to reclaim politics for everyday Americans. It was a powerful conversation. Most circles I find myself in, the phrase Tea Party gets the same scrunched nose and raised eyebrow. Tea Party Patriots are often painted in a largely negative light by the left. Lawrence would seem to be a hundred and eighty degrees the opposite direction of Meckler. These two appear so diametrically opposed one wouldn't even find them sitting in the same room, let alone talking with each other. These two don't just debate and agree with some things; they are friends. The two spent an hour that morning talking about finding common values that unite traditionally divided groups. Why? Because whether you want to admit it or not, at some level most of us have underlying values in common. Our paths to adhering to them are just different.

When managing change, it is important to think about diversity and bridging differences by finding common ground. For this purpose, diversity is bringing to the table two seemingly opposing forces. Think of Mark and Lawrence, or a chief officer from Wal-Mart sitting down with a food justice activist. We're going to need one heck of a bridge, right? Maybe that bridge just needs to be built with a whole lot of curiosity and understanding. Begin by asking what do each of us care about. Try to use value words from that answer to build into a new question. The questions need to be respectful, thought-provoking, and authentic. For example, maybe the question is framed: What are your thoughts on living wages for families? And not, why don't you pay living wages? There is an art to asking intentional and powerful questions. It is something that is worth planning. Here are some sample questions: What's important to you about (your specific situation) and why do you care? What's taking shape? What are you hearing underneath the variety of opinions being expressed? If there was one thing that hasn't yet been said to reach a deeper level of understanding, what would that be? What would it take to create change on this issue? This is even more important when dealing with groups that have been pitted against each other for a long time and come to the table with judgment and hesitation. Use common values as a bridge, not a bypass. Opening conversations with these questions to find common values helps emphasize the importance of the issue. Starting conversations here does not mean avoiding difficult discussions where we may disagree. Use the shared values to show the importance in fulfilling those values for all. Doing so can move audiences into a frame of mind that is more solution-oriented and less mired in skepticism or disagreement.

A tactic that can aid this discussion of building bridges and finding common ground is separating people from the issues. Think about it: What made the conversation between Mark and Lawrence powerful? It wasn't necessarily what was being said. It was the issues and organizations they were connected to that made the conversation powerful. The inherent message was that if we let go of the associations and just listen to the person standing in front of us, we might just find common ground. By addressing the person and tabling the issue, or moving to the side what the corporation does that isn't liked, a new conversation can be had.

We know why we don't like, or severely disagree, with a certain person based on particular issues. We don't, however, know the person we are sitting with and she probably does not know us. We are trying to build a bridge, something that links us to the other person. You might be surprised to know that there are some common values that drive both individuals, just in different ways. When you are sitting down with an individual it is important to separate that person from the issue and the corporation one is associated with. The individual is not the problem. The person might help to promote what we see as the problem, but the person and issue are separate.

If we are holding space and working with very diverse people it becomes crucial to keep the issue and the person separated. Attacking the individual for the issue maintains the status quo of division. That person, including ourselves, is not the problem or solution. Before these types of encounters, we must clearly define the issue and then separate the other individual and ourselves from it. Here, we can finally allow space in our minds to ask meaningful questions that may find commonalities.

With all this being said, it is more powerful and sustainable to direct change at the group rather than the individual. This induces the phrase: It's not the person, but the problem. It's not the interests we have, but the positions we cling to. When we direct energy at the individual level we turn the issue from the problem to the individual, causing a defensive reaction. Moreover, the person is not the problem. Separate who people are from their behavior or actions. Define the problem as an "it." To create change, we don't yell at people saying what they are doing is wrong and to simply do it our way. Why? Because it is an attack or at least it feels that way. So naturally, I may become defensive, dig my heels in even harder, and decide that I'm not changing my ways. However, if instead one looks at the process without pointing any fingers, then one is much more likely to at least have a conversation about it. We are looking at why something isn't working, not why one is doing it a particular way.

At the same time, the individual is how we make an issue personal and matter. Change starts with the individual, with ourselves. So, we come upon a paradox. The problem should not focus on individuals, and yet, the individual is where we must begin. Change agents must talk to individuals, but not as if we are trying to change that person. We talk to them as if we are trying to change the problem. Leave out the actions of the person who might stoke the problem or how you may feel that they promote what you see as the wrongs. The others' actions have little to do with your opinions and everything to do with their own perceptions of what the problem is and how to fix it. Both can have the same reasons for believing that each is in the right and the other in the wrong. Talking as if the blame lay on that individual is typically not going to get him to change, but only create heel-digging.

We begin to think how the problem might be the solution here. Once we start imagining the overlaps of networks, sparks can begin to ignite and then we can actively generate new and unheard-of associations. The overlap of networks is where each sector bumps up against the one next to it and where these associations can happen.

People across time have come together to inquire into differences, through which commonalities are found, and ultimately become united. In fact, getting a whole system in the room depends in some way on differences in a system. We are asked to point out these differences and leverage them to our advantage, not to shun them. Differences are inherent and if we allow them to issue forth we can find out that the system doesn't have to be negative and exhausting with opponents at every corner, but a source of creativity and learning. You might be surprised what you have in common with someone labeled the opponent. Better yet, the differences themselves are what make a system complete, interesting, and regenerative. Differences spark new ideas and patterns and can even aid in shifting paradigms.

As we move through different elements of communication, we will invariably find ourselves faced with the idea of the enemy or opponent. Fighting against something tends to get you further from motivation while fighting for something can increase one's motivation. Viewing someone or something as an opponent may help drive a campaign initially, but it doesn't supply sustenance and sustainability. For one, we have to keep up the hate to maintain the motivation, which will only remain for a limited time. Secondly, negativity just gets old. We are surrounded by it in the news, and advocates on any side who portray the other as the evil one must be stopped. The greater sustainable-agriculture community seems to be always fighting something, urging others to be issues oriented, to "take sides," and to consider their food purchase to be a political statement, when all the average consumer usually wants is to simply make a choice that reflects a positive, happy, trouble-free lifestyle. The general public can begin to feel overwhelmed and tired of being lectured and warned of yet another imminent crisis. On the other hand, most of the companies that are railed against do the exact opposite. They are constantly portraying a positive image and place. Now, some might say their stories are lies, but it does work. These companies don't spend time painting an enemy; they just keep bringing to the fold data and research to prove their point. Opponents call them liars or evil people and show the consequences of their actions. Which one do you think is going to work? Instead of polarizing and creating an enemy, change agents could talk about what to create. A focus on the creative solutions taking place is happening, and I'm seeing this more and more. It needs to be taken further. Labeling enemies can be unproductive in that it quickly turns into a battle where there are winners and losers. All we're trying to do is beat the opponent, forgetting altogether why we might have started this battle in the first place. Furthermore, if we are to view someone or something as an enemy, why wouldn't the opponent view us in the same light? Even if we think we're in the right as to how something should be done, the other side will naturally feel the same way. It is a defense mechanism that almost always surfaces when something has become a competition. Is that what this is, a competition? Is our food system simply a competition and we're just trying to win?

Capability Two: Communication

What if the enemy was transformed into just another person in this world with a different perspective? He wasn't someone to pin the whole wrongs of the system, rather someone to find common ground. No longer can we use language such as opponent, enemy, or uncommon bedfellows. This starts the conversation all wrong because that means we are already walking in seeing the other as a person who needs to be convinced of our way.

We've become so divisive, even within groups in the food system, it's time we look at what's similar first so we can appreciate the differences. Currently, differences aren't truly appreciated, especially issue-based differences. Unless we agree on the same issues, we can't speak to each other. This is the problem of not separating the issue from the person. Instead, we tend to blend the two together, making the issue define the person. However, it is exactly the opposite. We define the issues. Until we see this, we will continue to divide and separate ourselves from potentially amazing partnerships. Why not look at this with curiosity instead? Why not find out how we see the issue differently and why. Take a leap and attempt to truly understand the other's point of view.

While we are searching for common ground we must always be observing what is waiting to take shape. It cannot be stressed enough that collaboration must be done with a wide spectrum of people with differing opinions and beliefs. Ultimately, when shifting paradigms, you will be most likely creating disturbances in other people's experiences and receive resistance. You must look at managing these polarities where you are ready for change and, at the same time, are trying to reduce resistance. They are experiencing a disturbance that they may not understand. It's important to keep in mind that people will need time to get to the same place as you and start working on change. You must work at keeping them all engaged through finding that common ground. Move the people to change and implement the laws. Change the laws, change the culture. Change the culture, change the agenda.

Let's stop here and say more about management as opposed to resolution. A fundamental point in sustained change is managing diverse viewpoints. Real change does not come from trying to convince someone of my views. This typically creates more of that reactionary polarity, ultimately keeping you distanced from the other. The point is to create space where people can all exist and work toward common goals and visions eventually merging the resistant with the ready. This takes us right into dissecting conflicts and polarity. Think about pundits on either side of the mainstream political structure. Each one stands in direct opposition to the other and yet is also drawn to each other with a kind of magnetism. Each feed off the other really. What would happen if either side just stopped attacking the other? Power and energy would be taken away from the one still talking. The magnetic pull would cease to exist, but it seems that either side is too full of fear. One possible reason for this fear to stop is that each may be made the fool while the other side continues to bash. This theory of both sides stopping can seem counterintuitive. As one political pundit harangues another, the attacked feels he must return the proclamation further solidifying the conflict and polarity. In some cases, the conflict and polarity even intensify.

This happens among change agents as well. We exert more and more force on to who we deem as our opponents, expecting at some point for them to change. It is useful in some cases, like raising the cost of tomatoes at Trader Joe's so that tomato pickers in Florida can get paid better wages. Why doesn't this work all the time? Sometimes the movement does not have the necessary tipping point and sometimes we polarize too much. This creates a great deal of friction, making people feel attacked and ultimately getting stuck in the reinforcement cycle. The more change agents push, the more the opponent digs in her heels. It can create a pretty severe *us* versus *them* relationship. If continued, this becomes the base and normative of the relationship and how the two interact with one another. The conflict itself is what defines the relationship creating identities around it so that the very idea of this conflict ever being resolved cannot exist. I believe this to happen unconsciously, as most change agents work toward resolving a struggle. And yet, the dynamics that occur create the opposite field of experience where the existence depends on the struggle.

The thing with polarity is that it already exists quite naturally in the world. We don't need to go around creating more of it or intensifying what is already there. Polarity and paradox are part of that natural and magical component of life. It is the stuff that makes the following statement true. You will eventually get everything you want, but not at the time you want it, and not in the order you expect it. Taoism is the closest example of this mysticism. The *Tao Te Ching* is full of paradox and polarity. Act without acting, persuade without force, lead without leading are all examples. When first read, it can make little sense of how that's accomplished. It is in these ironic moments that make a person remark, "Of course." Polarity always exists whether we like it or even notice it. It's how the universe balances everything out. Though the universe doesn't always balance the way we might think it should be done. What I mean is that it is balanced in a paradoxical way. The two political pundits balance each other with their rhetoric. If one stopped, there would be an imbalance. Something would have to change so that it is balanced once again. It is precisely this reactionary polarity that provides incredible room for shifts and interventions. Everything has an equal opposite. If one politician stopped the reactions, or the whole party, then the other party would somehow shift in response because that polarity would be gone. A new balance would have to be found. This is just an example, but it is during that time of searching for a new balance where social change can happen. It's that decisive moment. It's removing the self-imposed polarities that are preventing sustained change from taking place.

Seeing where the polarizations are within the system will also shed light on patterns. The constant reactions that reinforce the polarities are patterns of behavior and understanding that ultimately turns into leverage for change. Even more, understanding and identifying these polarities and their patterns is exactly how the whole system is recognized. We find our opposites and then we sit down together to find if there is indeed something we share in common.

A key statement to remember is that resistance is something that "does not exist. It is attraction to an existing pattern."[9] Seeing patterns is crucial in the beginning stages of social change in any system. Without being aware of patterns, there is not enough knowledge to understand the system. This takes time and careful observation—and maybe most importantly—quite a bit of patience. What are the patterns within the distribution and growing systems? Where are the polarities that maintain these patterns? Remember, resistance is attraction to an existing pattern. The two political pundits are always dueling it out. Do they vehemently resist each other because of the tendency toward existing patterns? Then these patterns reinforce the polarized relationship. Once something becomes a habit, we are drawn to those existing patterns almost inherently. These patterns help to reinforce negative and positive relationships.

Identifying and working with polarity, and its patterns, is about creatively managing the tension between individuals not ready or unwilling for change and individuals who are ready. Something else to keep in mind is that those in power want to maintain the current beliefs that are beneficial to them. This goes for anyone in power who wants things to stay the same, if not for any other reason than that it is benefiting them. You don't know that something isn't working, if it always seems to be working for you. In very simplistic terms, this makes sense. If a new group rises to power, it may also try to maintain it by controlling beliefs unless this way of being is relinquished. To keep social power, you don't ask about other cultures or diversity. Power is not necessarily about a set of actions, but rather a set of cultural beliefs and definitions. This is a polarity that we should learn how to manage. Tension holding is about harnessing naturally occurring contradictions within the relationship or system to understand and speak to all the different views and draw everyone together. Below is a chart adapted from Barry Johnson's book *Polarity Management*.[10]

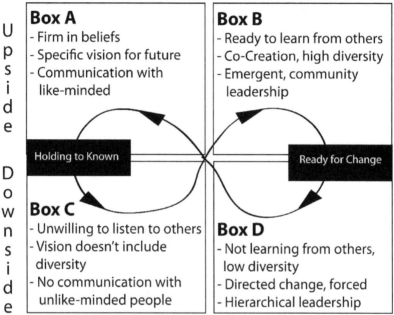

(Graphic adapted from *Polarity Management*, Barry Johnson.)

For this exercise, let us say that the left column represents the individual who is holding on to what she knows. This can be either Monsanto (a seller of seeds, fertilizers, and pesticides) believing what it knows to be true or La Via Campesina (a peasant-led movement of smallholder farmers) doing the same. The right column is the group or change agent who is ready for change. Boxes A and B represent the positive outcomes or upsides for focusing on each side in the top row. Boxes C and D represent the negative outcomes or downsides from focusing only on the bottom row while neglecting the top. Seeing all four of these boxes allows one to see the whole picture. The arrows in the chart demonstrate the flow of the social dynamics at play. This process, at its core, supports and gives voice to diverse viewpoints and manages fears, anxieties, and apprehension around the change effort. It visually shows the management of different needs as opposed to resolving them.

Learning how one shifts between these contradictions can seem hopeless. How does a change agent move through this grid so that each side is being included? "…it is the art of balancing opposites in such a way that they do not cancel each other but shoot sparks of light across their points of polarity. It looks at our desperate either/or and tells us they are really both/ands…"[11] Instead of looking at the system and saying it's either small farms or large farms, family farms or corporate farms, or some other dichotomy in the food system, we look and say it's both. Who knows what the solutions will be, but the current discussions to move through a sustainable change of the food system requires all the polarities to be present and to feel welcomed. It requires the contradictions and polarized relationships to be in the same room. Balancing polarities and moving through the above grid requires letting go of dichotomous behavior and attitudes and fostering inclusiveness and curiosity. The change agent, then, must be looking at how to pull everyone along, even those we disagree with. How might this be done? Listening. Listening to the individuals' needs, fears, and values that are emerging between the words. Here in this space, we will find the keys to our common ground and the baby steps to moving forward together. Because of how polarized many of the relationships have become in the food system, moving through this management will not be a walk in the park. Conflict-management skills will be necessary, as will a resoluteness to continually invite all system players in the community to the table.

A few things stand out here that are worth pointing out and delving into. First, it stands clearly that identifying patterns is essential and valuable. Finding these patterns lets us see the details. Think of the pattern on a leaf. It is the same pattern repeated, like a fractal. Fractals appear everywhere in nature. It is a pattern that reveals the minutest details. This is what can happen within social change as well. Seeing the patterns within our food distribution, or within our food and environmental system, or within our labor and food system reveal beautiful and telling details that help inform us of the greater whole. It helps us see the whole forest and the leaves. Furthermore, patterns are about finding a combination of acts or tendencies through locating commonalities among and between us. Truly that is how we pull and cycle through the polarity grid. We don't get people to move from holding to their existing patterns to holding onto new patterns by force and not caring about their feelings. We get people to move, and feel moved, by uncovering what and why each is holding on in the first place. This is tantamount. The only way to get people behind change is to fully listen and engage them in the process. It is in this space that we learn about the other and maybe something about ourselves. Maybe we even learn something new about what the food system should encompass. Over and again, I have found myself in group scenarios where if I hadn't made sure to listen to and engage each person, the project would have either fallen flat or been made difficult by other members.

Other elements that stand out are diversity and integration. By diving into the heart of polarity, we also begin to see how this values diversity and integrates rather than segregates individuals. It is all too easy to think that someone is so completely different that she shouldn't be included. We'll make a new food system without her! Can we really? By segregating whoever off while we go and make some beautiful alternative food system, is like creating our own little Omelas. It is not as extreme as a child in a closet suffering for our happiness. Yet, there is a sort of suffering that is placed upon any group that is simply left behind and out. Not to mention it is almost a fake kind of happiness we will have created in our wonderful sustainable food system. It is fake because it is not truly representative of all actors in the system. It is only representative of a few, much like the current system. Many change agents tout diversity and inclusion and yet at the same time practice uniformity and segregation to covet and protect their ideas. Everyone must be included in the new food system — and that means everyone. Currently, we have a balancing act happening. On one side, we have industrial agriculture and on the other we have agroecological agriculture. These two philosophies are diametrically opposed. Some believe that these two simply can't play together. Others do not want to play together for very real reasons. Our constant pushing further polarizes us and is simply wasting energy and preventing change. Agroecology is built upon the thesis of environmental diversity. For the most part, we understand that a healthy environment in nature is a diverse one. Yet, paradoxically, we do not practice this philosophy in other environments. We try to make everyone think the same exact way about the food system.

To stretch the brain in new ways, take Monsanto and pair it with an organization that seems disparate from it like La Via Campesina. The less the two seemingly have in common the better. Now, try to work out a way that these two could have a partnership if common ground was found. La Via Campesina exists in South and Central America with factions in Africa and India. Monsanto, traditionally viewed as part and parcel of industrial farming, has been involved with the green revolutions in India and Africa. Both involve farmers and work in the same geographic areas mainly in opposition to each other. These two groups are staged against each other rather obviously and so it may be difficult to see what a collaboration would be like between the two, but what could happen if these two found a way to work together? Who knows what it could look like or what form it would take given the differences. These two are so diametrically opposed that it's hard to imagine them working together in the slightest. Yet, they both work within agriculture. Could they collaborate on promoting and facilitating localized farmer innovations? This type of stretch requires assumptions to be left at the door and for organizations to potentially think differently about how they offer their services. It's this very situation that makes it ripe with potential creativity if ever given the chance. This is polarity management.

At a workshop on asking powerful questions, we were invited to get into groups based on four types of questions. I chose the group on building bridges. We were to share a real-life story to try and ascertain questions to take back with us. I decided to figure out how to have a conversation between someone from the corporate offices at Wal-Mart and an individual from a food justice organization. I gave context to the group on why this would even be a concern. To my amazement, I felt the immense weight of how hard this is to do. I went in thinking in my head that the questions just need to be intentional and respectful. But when I found myself acting it out with my group, I came up blank. After a long period of reflection on this event, I realized that the one key aspect that was blocking my ability to act out the above sequence was assumptions. These will get you every time and completely block an honest process. I was making assumptions toward the activist and the Wal-Mart executive, which prohibited me from thinking clearly and honestly. Any assumptions, no matter how right you think they are, must be parked at the door to generate creative collaboration. Building bridges is not going to be a walk in the park. It needs to be truly desired, not simply done for show, if it is to work. We need to ask questions, drop our assumptions, and think not just about our own interests and issues, but those of the others as well. Where do they begin to overlap and where might we find common values?

Our beliefs and underlying assumptions are where the change needs to be if it is to be systemic. It is our paradigms that keep us where we are at. It is the things we believe in that make us do what we do. Beliefs are what make up our culture—these are the things that control the agenda. Earlier it was noted that the political system is driven by our culture. Here, it comes bubbling up again. Culture is driving our agenda. There are lots of factions that try to moderate our culture and the paradigms we operate from. At the end of the day, it is our culture that sets the agenda. This is important and cannot be stressed enough. To create any sustained change, we must get at the underlying assumptions we believe to be true. We must get at these, not to tell people that they are wrong or should believe something else, but to find ways of accessing these people so that we can learn different ways of knowing and understanding the world around us. This is the long-term answer. One that we can move toward, but it will take a great amount of time to shift these. It is like an iceberg. The piece showing above water looks almost small and insignificant. Peering down under the water, however, shows the base of the iceberg at four to five times the size of the top. It is that bottom part of the iceberg that we need to move to shift paradigms. No small task. It can be done.

Up until now, most of what has been written focuses on interacting with the other, but we also need to focus on ourselves. There are two ways that this happens: one is self-regulation and the second is accepting feedback. These two are not mutually exclusive. In Taoism, self-regulation alludes to moderating one's control and cultivating the center. Too much control conceives an ideal outcome and attempts to restrict concepts and people into that ideal. Avoiding extremes and confrontational postures is the key to self-regulation. The more I do something, the more its polarity will appear—a kind of reinforcing loop. The grid in polarity management illustrated this with the differing quadrants where boxes A and D are balanced extremes as are B and C. Individuals will naturally move into the opposite quadrants when too much control is exerted. In *The Tao of Leadership*, John Heider states that, "The best group process is delicate. It cannot be pushed around. It cannot be argued over or won in a fight. The leader who tries to control the group through force does not understand group process. Force will cost you the support of the members."[12] One must self-regulate to monitor one's force by accepting feedback and cultivating one's center. Accepting feedback is rather obvious in its meaning. The individual leader must listen to others, internalize it, and have that feedback become part of the whole. Cultivating one's center involves listening more than speaking, to be aware of the process, to reflect, and to be still. Additionally, being centered is knowing where you stand and what you stand for while remaining flexible when bringing in other views and positions.

Self-regulation requires individuals to keep a watchful eye on the decisive moment and to moderate our own control and center within groups. Furthermore, by maintaining a center, one can provide solid sense-making during this perceived chaos of change. Both self-regulation and accepting feedback allow the change agent to stabilize the various forms of voices within change. Accepting feedback removes one from the expert-driven culture and asks us to lead as a facilitator. Lastly, this kind of feedback acceptance allows for our own cultural history as well as the multifarious cultural opinions and views of others to coexist within the system. Self-regulation is key to a healthy system. Keep feedback coming, keep different viewpoints stirring, and be open to being changed yourself!

The Illusion of Separation

What may be going through your head at this point is that this all sounds well and good, but there is no way people with extremely different viewpoints will sit in a room to learn from each other, while at the same time staving off any assumptions they might have about the other. As we know, there are many varied stakeholders in the food system and we disagree all the time. To make matters worse, there are trust issues between groups that have demonized each other. These problems cannot be resolved through regular, linear problem-solving that we may be used to. Systemic interest pushes individuals to a state of collaboration where we are socially constructing the path together. It's a rough road. However, this route negotiates a new path where the incompatible outlooks become a strength not a weakness. Find out what is driving each of us in our work. Why do we do what we do? It is here that we can begin to transcend our differences. Remember that we are not solving problems but balancing polarities. Defining the problem by identifying the perfect question is the first step in locating the solutions.

Cloke and Goldsmith, authors of *Resolving Conflicts at Work*, state that the "deepest truth is that there is no separation between ourselves and our opponents, other than the illusion that what separates us matters and is unbridgeable."[13]

4   Capability Three: Reflection in Action

The insistence that the oppressed engage in reflection on their concrete situation is not a call to armchair revolution. On the contrary, reflection – true reflection – leads to action.

— *Paulo Freire*

In this culture, we are typically measured on how fast we can get things accomplished. The faster you are, the more accolades you acquire. In the advocate world, there seems to be so much doing that they miss out on the reflection and observation components. They're moving on to the next action or the next meeting that discusses the timeline for the next action. Given our political climate at times, it can also feel that this is what advocates should be doing. There's no time for taking time out to reflect. Paulo Freire used critical thinking as a nonviolent approach to revolutionary change first in Brazil and then in many other countries. He fomented power in poor communities just by getting them to critically think, observe, and reflect, much like the group-learning theorists mentioned earlier.

Capability Three: Reflection in Action

Managing change means that we must also be observant. This is similar to a Taoist phrase of act without acting. Act with intention, not force, while being with whatever is happening by harmonizing with the environment. If force is used frustration can surely follow, and from that, much wasted energy. Furthermore, it denotes being mindful of one's surroundings and to act in congruence with it. Congruence does not insinuate that we start agreeing with our surroundings. It means that we stop pushing so hard and employ less active tools. This could include listening, facilitating, and discussing with an open mind among many options. As change agents, we can constantly be in a retaliation mode, reacting constantly. This can sometimes be the opposite of act without acting that gives rise to exhaustion and burnout. But, as Freire and many others point out, we need to give real priority to strategically and critically thinking about ourselves, our behavior and actions, and our culture to manifest sustained change. When we pull back and look at the whole of the system and not just its individual pieces that we are working on, we are tasked with great adaptive challenges where swift action could lead to demise. At times, we need to resist the pressure to do something and spend more time reflecting on our behavior and actions while also listening to others. Even if this feels like the antithesis of what we know and have been taught.

Reflection in action is the ability to improvise and be adaptable and agile in the moment while also prompting reflection among others and within a group. It also includes being able to recognize the gaps between people's believed theory and their theory-in-use to help them understand and act upon those differences. This is knowing and trusting in oneself to maintain your center. Reflection in action requires deep attention and awareness. At its core, one must be able to reflect in the present moment and then integrate the resulting insights into your actions.

What distinguishes this type of reflection from other modes of reflection is the inherent action that must take place. Most times when we think of reflection, we think of taking time out to think about what happened in the past and how it could be improved for the future when we stumble into a similar situation. Reflection in action is thinking about what is happening while it is presently taking place and then modifying your actions or behavior in the moment based on this in-the-moment reflection. An excerpt from Schon portrays this nicely:

> When good jazz musicians improvise together, they similarly display reflection in action smoothly integrated into ongoing performance. Listening to one another, listening to themselves, they "feel" where the music is going and adjust their playing accordingly. A figure announced by one performer will be taken up by another, elaborated, turned into a new melody. Each player makes online inventions and responds to surprises triggered by the inventions of the other players. But the collective process of musical invention is organized around an underlying structure. There is a common schema of meter, melody, and harmonic development that gives the piece a predictable order. In addition, each player has at the ready a repertoire of musical figures around which he can weave variations as the opportunity arises. Improvisation consists in varying, combining, and recombining a set of figures within a schema that gives coherence to

the whole piece. As the musicians feel the directions in which the music is developing, they make new sense of it. They reflect in action on the music they are collectively making—though not, of course, in the medium of words.[14]

At many a workshop, I have rearranged the sequence of my agenda, changed the amount of time spent on an exercise, and even completely omitted exercises from the agenda all during facilitating. I have modified questions, and in some cases, have almost thrown the entire prepared presentation away and just started improvising with what I was reading in the room. That last one was just about the biggest reflection in action I've done yet. It was my third workshop in one community on the same topic. Each workshop was working to move the group ever closer to building new initiatives at their programs. I had spent nine months holding monthly calls with the group, as well as individual coaching calls, surveys, and two previous workshops. We knew what the agenda needed to be without a doubt. That is, until I got to the meat of the workshop and opened it up with my question that I posed with full excitement and expectation. They all just stared at me. No one made a sound. They also didn't seem to follow what I was asking. I backed up, explained what I wanted the group to do and repeated the question in a different way. Nothing. Pure silence. At this point, my mind was already reeling at what I was observing and how I was going to turn it around so it would be an effective workshop for the participants. However, even though I was reflecting in action, nothing was coming to mind and I just knew I couldn't continue to push this agenda. So, I sat down my agenda notes and said, "Okay, what do you want to talk about?" I told them that I want this time to be useful for them. We rebuilt the agenda for that afternoon right then and ended up having an inspiring conversation. As a designer and facilitator, one must harness the skill of creatively responding to change. Like anyone wanting to create change, I first sit down and create the design and flow of a workshop. I create a layout of each exercise and think about what might come up that I should be aware of and create small plan B's for each exercise where possible. However, there is no way to know all that may or may not happen once the workshop begins as I've learned. That depends on the dynamics that unfold within the group. While preparing the agenda, a mantra I continue to repeat in my head is that *whatever happens is what needs to happen* and that I must relinquish all expectations of what I would like to see happen minus maybe some broad goals of why the workshop is happening in the first place. If I want the people in the workshop to own what happens, then I cannot control it or dictate it. Up until the day of the workshop, the most control I exert and have any power over is the agenda itself. However, if I'm staying alert to the group dynamics, I also know that once I set foot into the workshop even my agenda becomes a living document up for changes at any given moment.

There are some workshops where I do completely control the agenda. But there are many where the agenda shouldn't be controlled by one person or organization much like my example. I feel that workshops, if about social change, should be led by the group. I merely facilitate them toward the change by holding the space. I plan an agenda based on my knowledge of how best to get groups moving and talking, while at the same time I remain completely open to what unfolds in the moment and fully prepared to modify my agenda as needed. I am responding in the moment to intended and unintended consequences of the exercises. I am also reflecting in action; I'm not operating on autopilot by following the agenda word for word. This requires honing skills that help one read a room, understand group dynamics, the ability to relinquish control and personal desired expectations and most importantly, to remain flexible.

There is something that can get in the way of reflection, and that's knowing in action. This is the process in which we know how to design something. For instance, I've facilitated many workshops, so I have knowledge around what typically does and doesn't work. Knowing in action happens without conscious deliberation. It's the autopilot that can turn on when you've done something many times. When something takes us by surprise it is because something has happened that falls outside of these knowns or routine. It interrupts our knowing in action so that we must reflect in action. It is jarring and more times than not can easily be brushed aside as some anomaly. But this surprise is exactly what is jolting us into the present moment and turning off the autopilot. This surprise can give rise to on-the-spot experimentation, creative sparks, and inspiring conversations.

Reflecting also gives rise to points of intervention, which no matter the type, should be done with care and strategy. I can't just intervene wherever and whenever and expect others to simply fall into place. Frustration and exhaustion will surely follow. It is not about what I want and when and how I want it. If we want to see change, it is about what the system is ready for and being ready to leverage that at any given moment. We can only recognize these if we are being observant and reflecting in the moment. Once when I worked on a farm, we were performing an intense search and rescue of water-logged tomatoes. We were picking them early to protect them from bursting at the seams. In this experience, we couldn't make tomatoes ripen any faster than the natural process, but they can ripen in different scenarios. When there is too much rain, we can pull them off the vine early and ripen them in the sun. The tomatoes can also ripen on the vine, the traditional way. Either process, whether on the vine or not, takes however long it's going to take. I can't force the tomatoes to go any faster. I can help them in the different phases with a subtlety of tension and pressure, meaning that I can influence. This can serve as a metaphor for humans as well.

How do we locate points of intervention and leverage them like the tomatoes? Discovery happens through observation and identifying patterns. Our goal is to observe and listen to what is happening around us. Notice the patterns in the system and identify disturbances for these become key intervention points. These points are typically small, yet they become big sea changes when all the small acts begin to converge. Our individual acts of change may seem small but they are significant. To shift the culture, we need many small acts happening all the time. It is about making the personal political, and about moving from an observer to an active participant. A former graduate professor said once: "It is about drying your bags in public." He was referring to cloth vegetable storage bags that would literally dry outside so people would see them. He was asking us to make public our beliefs, to metaphorically dry our bags in public. What would that look like?

There's a story about a Lakota shawl dance. A young, female tribal basketball player, who faced a hostile anti-Indian crowd, performed a shawl dance before the basketball game began. It reversed the crowds' hostility. Another story spoke of the courage it took to march in the streets over thirty years ago for a gay man, lesbian, or transgender. They spoke of the dangerous risk to march, but that also to not march was another kind of risk. "A risk that leaves you with no name, half-dead, and unremembered."[15] Yet another story was of a Unitarian church holding an evening forum to share how they were feeling after 9/11. There was a man there who worked in a corporate setting. He said that he had heard the story about the girl doing the shawl dance in front of a hostile crowd. After hearing the story, he went to work, where he is a manager, and placed a small four-inch American flag upside down on the outside of his cubicle. He said it was his shawl dance and that the invitation to resistance is a sacred offering and every day we make our own responses to it. So go for it, air those bags in public all you can. Actions done in the solitude of your home won't cut it. We also need brave public acts.

Change is relentless incrementalism. It has been revealed that we never know which small act will push us to that tipping point. Instead of looking for ways to make huge sea changes, seek out small actions that are effective in their own way much like my community meetings eventually building a coalition. Until change hits that climax it is fragmented. There are all these small, and not so small acts, happening around the globe. On some level, there is similarity because they are pushing the same cause, for example, farmers and farm workers' rights. This is fragmented change, a similar and repetitious act of change happening around the globe making a pattern. Incremental change actions are what civil-rights activists were doing. A pattern was created that repeated itself until it became one pattern and one voice of change.

All this is to say that we should commit to tiny acts of courage every day. This can be attending a community meeting, social justice book club, rally, protest, or boycott. It can also simply be holding space for someone while they speak. Even the smallest of small acts works toward moving us through the social change cycle. Whether it's drying your bags in the front yard, a meaningful dance in front of a hostile group, an upside down American flag at your desk, political art, or a simple conversation with someone you have differing opinions with. As change agents, this is what we are trying to get people to do. Our goal is to move us through that cycle of social change to end up with new structures in place.

I think it is easy for us to overlook the small because of wanting change now. However, small and gradual allows time for observation and interaction with different ideas as well as reflection. I have two examples of how this practice helps us see the significantly small and important acts. There was a workshop hosted at a King County library that I facilitated on food justice. We were all hyped for a huge crowd. How many people showed up? Three. I could have seen that as a failure and if attendance was all I cared about, I suppose it did fail. However, one participant was a student at the local university and was writing a paper on Food Sovereignty. He had many questions and was very interested. He was there with his mother who was just as inquisitive. The mother even asked questions around what she can do in her daily life to help make a difference. After the workshop, I gave multiple additional resources to the son. The third participant was someone who worked at the local Darigold facility and had personal, firsthand accounts to offer us. These three made the workshop a success in my eyes. The mother and her son were now two more people armed with knowledge and passionate enough about it to feel they could talk with friends and family. For the change agent, this is small and effective change. Who knows what ripple effects came from that encounter. Size doesn't matter; it's what you do with what you have in front of you.

My second example is from when I lived in Indiana. I found myself with a mentor who believed in an idea I had in forming a new coalition that would be comprised of food, labor, health, and governmental organizations and work toward food justice. To kick-start the whole thing, John and I held community meetings at a local activist coffee shop and church. We had standing meetings every month. John and I were there like clockwork to facilitate and help move the projects and mission forward. The attendance varied month to month with one meeting having only one person showing up. I was new to organizing, and in that moment, I felt completely dejected and wanted to cry. I brought up in the first few minutes that maybe this just wasn't working. Then the one person who came looked at me and said how important my constant presence was to everyone. She said that there was stability in knowing that every month, at this time and on this day, I would be here waiting for whoever showed up. I was someone the other group members could count on, and if I stopped holding the meetings, the coalition would fall apart. Who knew that my important act was just holding space every month? That seemed like an insignificant act and it was small, but it was important to moving the coalition forward. That moment humbled and transformed me.

Reflection can also allow time to recuperate and manage our personal capacities. As activists, this is really important. We tend to burn the candle at both ends, sometimes leading to pessimism and total burnout. Honoring our energy and capacity helps us think clearly and strategically, as well as provides time to reflect and observe whether we are still on the path we want to be on. Remember, observation and reflection is one of the first steps in the social change cycle and continues throughout it.

This makes the most important response component to change as act without acting. Rather than constantly trying to fight, we can simply maintain the base of our story and definition. Act without acting asks us to be with the moment, move with it, and leverage it. For example, when power-holders began to strip social safety nets in the 1980s, advocates could have included these legislative matters as a broader definition of antipoverty. Instead of renaming, they could have maintained the name and broadened the definition and story, which will be talked about more in chapter five. Act without acting would have been just this. It's staying centered and true amid rough currents.

This skill of nonaction helps to highlight points of intervention. These points are like decisive moments where there is leverage to potentially create change — whether big or small. If you are paying attention to the surroundings enough, you will notice this moment when it is happening and can grab hold of it. This takes patience, vigilance, observation, and reflection. This is no different in social change or any kind of change for that matter. If one is paying attention and being involved in the present moment, then she will notice moments that are opportunities to give rise to oneself. You can feel the moments coming in the seconds beforehand. It is an intuition, a gut instinct, that a fork in the road is appearing and a decision will be made, even if that decision is to do nothing with that moment. There is a right time and place for action. Nonaction means to be observant of these potential points where change could be leveraged. This is not to say that we need to accept potential atrocities that are happening in the world or our communities. On the contrary, we are gently prodding all the while and maintaining our base. These gentle prods can take many forms: rallies, book clubs, community meetings, protests, et cetera. These are all great tactics for rallying public support as we have seen with the United Farm Workers Union and many others. They all have a time and a place for intervening in change. After rallies and protests, at some point, groups on either side have to meet and listen to each other. Furthermore, as Donella Meadows, the lead author of *Limits to Growth*, stated, "We can't impose our will on a system. We can listen to what the system tells us, and discover how its properties and our values can work together to bring forth something much better than could ever be produced by our will alone."[16] This gets to the heart of change and nonaction. Our will plays out by flattening people to a two-dimensional stick figure or pushing what we think is right onto others without listening.

Reflecting can also be uncomfortable. As we observe we begin to see possibilities and impossibilities. Reflecting shines light on gaps between what we thought was happening and what is actually happening. While these become points of intervention, they can also become overwhelming points. In many of my experiences, down to the simplest meeting, the feeling of impossibilities abound. I face pushback not just over outcomes, but over the processes I believe in that others may find too inclusionary and arduous. I have more than once been asked, "Why don't you just tell them what you want to have happen?" In the face of this, how do we keep moving forward? Rudolf Bahro, an East German dissident, stated: "When the forms of an old culture are dying, the new culture is created by a few people who are not afraid to be insecure."[17] Bahro is saying that feeling groundless and unsure, maybe even lost, can be helpful if we can sit in it without fleeing the scene. It's difficult to stand still while one feels insecure. I have felt this exact moment a number of times and each time I call on my center. It isn't pleasant—sitting in that moment, but I have come to terms with this feeling, its uncomfortableness, anxiety, and awkwardness even. I have learned to not feel helpless or run from the scene no matter how much I may want to. Instead I find my center and drive my ship through the stormy waters being mindful all the way.

Reflection in Action Overview

Reflection in action is thought and action happening together. It is adaptive and coevolving with the present moment. When practicing, we do not get stuck in past events and patterns. We are looking objectively at what is taking place in front of us and responding to present moments inspiring innovation. This requires active listening toward those around you without judgment or assumptions. If we let our judgments come into play, we are no longer in the present moment, but in the past and responding based on the past and not the present.

Reflection in action can be the spawn of social construction. Creativity comes from thoughtful social reflection on the events that we experience. This process can also be called thinking on one's feet. It entails building new understandings to inform our actions in the situation that is unfolding.

"The practitioner allows himself to experience surprise, puzzlement, or confusion in a situation which he finds uncertain or unique. He reflects on the phenomenon before him, and on the prior understandings which have been implicit in his behaviour. He carries out an experiment which serves to generate both a new understanding of the phenomenon and a change in the situation." [18]

5   Capability Four: Cocreation

Real movement begins with vision — with inspiration and engagement, with a pull and not a push.

— Anthony Weston

This book is about direction and purpose. The ideas are bold and intentional. The ask is deliberate: to put our weight behind these ideas and dedicate ourselves to true change and collaboration. We can say we foster leadership, and that we work toward social change, and that we are changing the system, and that we are collaborators, but what does that matter? Those are just words. What matters are our actions. What matters is achieving social change that will not happen if we let the divisiveness of our culture prevail. If we feed into it and divide ourselves for the glory at the end of the day, all we are left with is the glory and the ego. The problems are still there and not fixed. In the years I've worked in agriculture, activism, and hunger-relief, one constant has always remained: the ego. Each organization needs to be the one with the recognition. I've seen numerous collaborations and coalitions falter and crack under this weight. We lose sight of why we're here doing the work we're compelled to do. Each of us wants our organization to be the one doing it, the one that gets the credit, or the one that is ultimately controlling the agenda.

Competition and collaboration is a good place to start for it is a deep-seated problem that must be dealt with and discussed. Individuals and organizations tend to throw around the word "collaboration" without ever thinking about what that means. At the same time, each organization wants the funding and is scrambling to be first so that they obtain first credit for the program, idea, or whatever it may be. It seems the free-market economy has indeed wiggled its way into every facet of our culture, making competition a key component of our very nature. This must be undone and is no small task. It will require us to be brave, to put aside our trust issues without risking safety, and potentially be the first to begin tearing down the walls that have been cemented between some groups. There has indeed been a strong wall built over many years between food justice activists and corporations with many verified and reasonable trust issues. However, there can be a place where we do not forget this, but suspend it for a moment so that an intentional dialogue can take place.

Disparate and seemingly contradictory collaborators can create an environment of high collaboration and low competition between interdependent groups. This means pushing each other to new forms of collaboration where we are creating new movements and ideas with groups we may not have thought about working with. When thinking about the food system, everyone is a collaborator, and we are all dependent on each other even if we may not like one another. If we are to work with others who we may not like and have built a system around not liking each other, we must reduce our competitive nature. Low competition implies that we do not view others as competitors — or even enemies — rather it is an individual with a distinctive viewpoint or an organization that represents a distinctive viewpoint. This produces a creative spectrum and stretches us to think how we are collaborating with others.

Examples of some interdependent groups in the food system are processors, small farmers, food workers, industrial farmers, farm workers, food-retail companies, environmental justice organizations, food justice organizations, distributors, legislators, and foundations like Wal-Mart or Gates Foundation among many others. Whether we like it or not we are linked to each other. High collaboration and low competition means that we understand our collective impact and that we share in the same destiny whether we agree with each other or not. This is easier said than done for even within similar fields, like hunger-relief or sustainable agriculture, we find ourselves competing against each other for funding, credit of new programs, distributing more, reaching more, ad nauseam. Unfortunately, it is precisely this that causes exhaustion, burnout, and cynicism among activists and advocates alike. This is not collaboration. It may have a veneer of collaboration, as in, we are all fighting the same battle, but these individuals and organizations are not collaborating. Rather, we are stuck in a wheel of competition against each other fighting for money and credit. This only works to our demise for if we are already in competition within our respective fields, how will we ever be able to lower the competition bar with outside systems we rail against. And if we cannot put ego or self-righteous behavior to the side, this will not work because we won't be deeply listening to the other. There will be no generative or adaptive learning.

Further, if we are not willing to listen and adapt, why should the person sitting across from us?

What may be going through your head at this point is that this sounds all well and good, but there is no way people with extremely different viewpoints will sit in a room to learn from each other, while at the same time staving off any assumptions they might have about the other. There are some pretty serious trust issues between these groups that have demonized each other. If the stakeholders within a system have differing and potentially incompatible outlooks and interests, then they cannot be resolved through regular, linear problem-solving that we may be used to. Examples of such differing groups are the Gates Foundation, Wal-Mart, La Via Campesina, National Sustainable Agriculture Coalition, small-scale and industrialized farmers, Monsanto, AGRA Watch, and Vandana Shiva. The list goes on of supposedly incompatible outlooks. We need to round and skew that linear thinking and move from an individual-interest focus to a systemic-interest focus to find commonalities. As we know, there are many varied stakeholders in the food system. We disagree or share incompatible outlooks and answers. So, a linear route cannot be used to solve all the problems. Systemic interest pushes individuals to a state of collaboration where we are socially constructing the path together. It's a rough road; however, this route negotiates a new path where the incompatible outlooks become a strength not a weakness. This is the only way around differing and potentially incompatible viewpoints. It also infers that we will be changing paradigms, rewiring ourselves, others, and the whole system. This means that even though we will come up against people who disagree, we all have something to contribute. Furthermore, if we share incompatible outlooks, then we must dig deep and get to our underlying values. Find out what is driving each of us in our work. Why do we do what we do? It is here that we can begin to transcend our incompatibilities and paradigms. Here is where we start to work together and leverage our differences.

I read an article recently that highlighted a new kind of activist who makes friend of opponents and builds bridges between unlikely allies and issues. The few people who are highlighted in the article are doing the work that I believe more activists in the food system need to turn toward. What most struck me was that the beginning of the article talked of Saul Alinsky and his traditional approach. This includes seeing the opponent as an enemy and strategies like pressure and attack. While these are not bad, we must understand that every action causes a reaction. If someone throws a wrench, we react. I'm asking us to rethink what kind of wrench we have and how we plan on using it.

The universe is always balancing. If there is someone on the left who becomes extreme, then there will be someone on the right who will become extreme to balance it out. This happens quite naturally. There will always be at least two ways of seeing an issue and people to represent each side. It is called diversity of opinions and ideas. We should celebrate this when creating change. However, there are some opinions that shouldn't be celebrated, such as with racism, sexism, xenophobia, or homophobia. I'm speaking to a diversity of opinions on creating a new food system. These isms play a heavy role in our food structure and need to be addressed and challenged in the process of creating something new so that they are not continued. Outside of these opinions, do we want to live in a world where we all think the same way and agree on everything? I find opinions that I can't even wrap my brain around interesting, for the very reason that I can't fathom how one got there. That's interesting to me! How did they get there? Why do they think that way? I become the most curious person when I find myself around something I don't understand or agree with because I want to understand it and why that person believes in it. I may not ever agree with that person, but I at least want to understand her if possible. That's the beauty of diversity: learning about different views, beliefs, and opinions. This creates rich dialogue, learning and teaching opportunities, and hopefully partnerships and collaborations. Diversity is healthy in all scenarios of life, not just gardening and farming. Diversity is what's missing in the modern, industrial farmers' toolkit. It is why they deal with superweeds and superbugs. In organizational development, facilitators are asked to work across departments — to mix it up and bring those dichotomous worlds together. So why in the food system do we try to promote just one idea while bad-mouthing the other? That is an overgeneralization, but you get the point. The use of polarizing words keeps the two factions from never even meeting in the middle. It's as if they are natural, universal enemies who have been relegated to this position to balance one another out. Even though this may be a universal balance, we do have the power to change what the universe in balancing on each side of the teeter totter. We each can choose whether we are a friend or a foe. A friend would not think of anyone as a foe or enemy, but rather someone who has a different opinion and life experience. A foe would view the other as an enemy, call her such, and not be open to learning about her opinion and life experience. A foe maintains the current balance. A friend disrupts the balance to socially construct something new, potentially uncomfortable, and full of integrated diversity.

This divide also creates polarizing language. We need to move away from dichotomous words such as "enemy." All they do is continually get people pitted against each other. No one wants to partner with someone who labels them the "bad guy" or "enemy." Sounds like an abusive relationship if you ask me. These words are simple and yet continue the struggle. They maintain the status quo and develop the feeling of righteousness, which in its essence is feeding the ego. We need to shake up the status quo! We also need to realize that the universe works in complex yet simple ways.

After we have explored our potential lack of diversity and undermining polarizing language in our work, we move on to creating and testing alternatives that will lead to new understandings. It is precisely here that we need and use cocreation. As alternatives are successful (or not,) we form new understandings and new conventions. These new understandings and conventions lead to change in actions and behavior. This, in turn, creates new experiences that if the intention is being achieved, these new understandings become the new norms that are repeated and eventually become fixed. This is the process that happens with any social change. One of the most important pieces of this model is that it is experiential and requires integrated collaboration. It is not a process performed alone or even with only like-minded people. Each step mentioned: examining, reflecting, discovery, testing, and development of new understandings are all done within a group with dissimilar yet interested people.

How do we begin the work of true cocreation and what is it? Cocreation is the ability to involve all actors directly, and in some cases, repeatedly, from beginning to end to achieve a compelling purpose. It builds a shared vision by encouraging personal visions so a common group purpose can emerge. Cocreation asks us to hold creative tension and provide openness. In the spirit of this practice we build something new together, something that holds all our visions in a unified manner. Cocreation also requires the first three capabilities of holding space, communication, and reflection in action. There are three main possibilities in cocreation. One option is that two or more interacting groups change into one new thing; or they remain separate but changed; or they interact yet remain unchanged and separate. The first is where cocreation exists. The second is collaboration and the third is simply an interaction. It's transactional. All three can create change, yet one can see as you move from transactional to collaboration to cocreation that the change can become more sustainable and systemic.

We accomplish this through integrated collaboration. Who doesn't collaborate right? We all do on some level and would all easily call ourselves collaborators. But I beg to differ and offer up a spectrum of collaboration strategies. These will ask us to stretch our understandings. These are not my invention but rather borrowed from a former professor who teaches leadership to individuals from around the globe. There are the four styles of collaboration within this spectrum, each increasing in intensity: networking, coordinating, cooperating, and integrating.

Network is an arms-length collaboration. It requires reciprocity and connects people contractually or in a project-based way. Its relationship is limited in time and space. One can think of this as transactional. One does something in return for something else. There is little trust here. Coordination collaboration consists of sharing information. It moves up the scale from networking because it involves conversations. Exchanges are flowing more freely here. There is an increase in time needed and trust is built between the involved parties. The last two strategies take the most time and trust and contain the most complexity. They can also be highly rewarding with the shared destiny being the most inclusive of a system. Cooperative collaboration is hands-on where there is a sharing of resources and work so that codevelopment can happen. This style builds networks. The last style is integrative collaboration. It is the most intense requiring the most time, trust, and complexity. This is where new knowledge is cocreated for a shared destiny. Even though each spectrum increases with intensity, one is not better than another. There are times and places for each category of collaboration just as there is a time and place for each tool of change (protests, rallies, community meetings). For instance, arms' length and sharing information is more tactical collaboration like the WTO (World Trade Organization) protests in Seattle, Washington in 1999. Whereas, cocreating new knowledge showed itself in the Occupy Movement or in farmer-led documentation practices in the Global South. It is precisely this shared-destiny category of collaboration that I believe the food system needs to exist given its multitude of varying stakeholders. The meaning of integrative collaboration is exactly what we are called to do in changing the food system. We must cocreate new knowledge, socially reconstruct what the food system looks like, and it must have a collective impact to stick. It is full integration. The food system is too interconnected for anything less.

This is social reconstruction. Social construction always questions conventional wisdom. In situations of ambiguity and pressure, people will cling to existing understandings and routines. Cultural discontinuity is more likely to be resisted than a reinterpretation, which makes these models so important as it brings everyone along, meeting them where they are at. It becomes a new way of applying existing values and beliefs. A friend of mine has a great saying that social construction is like social construction paper. Construction paper is used for making models and designs. When done in a group atmosphere, it becomes social. Maybe we all need to embrace our inner child and get out the social construction paper and start drawing and folding.

Cultural competency is a component of cocreation and asks us to embrace diversity within opinions, paradigms, beliefs, cultures, ethnicities, orientations, desires, and truths. There are many different ways to build a food system and currently we are all fighting tooth and nail to be the one kind that rises to the top. For all the clamor of agroecology, which at its core is about increased diversity, many individuals paradoxically shut down to the thought of diverse opinions of the food system. Without a genuine approach to diversity, without the strength to have one's own opinions challenged and broadened, we all risk never creating change over the long term, but only moments in time where something different bubbled up and then dissipated. To the risk of our ego, we need to relinquish it by realizing that we are not always right. Your opinion is right and true for you, but not someone else. Without cultural competency, how will we ever pull the ones not ready for change into our sphere when managing polarities? How will we emerge leaders if we are not fostering differing opinions? How will we create that moment of disequilibrium and amplification that is critical in change if we hinder differing opinions? The expert-driven culture runs deep in the United States and prevents us from developing our competence and understanding toward those who are different. This will not be easy as has already been said. Cultural competency is not only a difference in how or when we were raised. It also brings into the fold structural racism and gender equality. These are tough issues that will have to be dealt with when managing different opinions and polarities. I think Senator Cory Booker sums it up very nicely on how we must interact with these issues:

> Let us be humble and do the difficult work
> of finding ways to collaborate and
> cooperate with those whose political
> affiliations may differ from ours.
>
> But let us never, ever, surrender, forfeit, or
> retreat from our core values, our fundamental
> commitments to justice over prejudice;
> economic inclusion over poverty and
> unmerited privilege; and, always, love over

hate. Let us speak truth to power; fiercely
defend those who are bullied, belittled,
demeaned or degraded; and tenaciously fight
for all people and the ideals we cherish.
        – Senator Cory Booker on Facebook

Public policy is deeply interconnected with the food system
and feeds the groundswell of change. It is also the best
example of how much cocreation is needed. Public policy is an
important part of social change and is the agreements we
make as a public. Policy is a collaborative process, and we
must be able to see where others are coming from to
successfully modify policies. We must be able to strategically
think and manage polarities, hold diverse opinions, lower
competition, and increase collaboration. In short, policy itself
must hold all four capabilities of holding space,
communication, reflection in action, and cocreation.
Inherently, public policy is socially constructed, defines how
we make decisions together, and takes massive collaboration
between many differing groups of people. It is incremental,
building on the past and toward the society we would like to
have. Policy represents our cultural values, mental models,

and expectations on the individual and collective levels, which is why diversity and cultural competency are so important. Changing inequitable practices is where public policy steps in. Policy exists to create new legislation and modify the old. This must be working in tandem with the work on the ground to effect change. Policy and activism do not happen independently of each other, in fact, they need each other. Much like the social change model presented earlier, policy follows a similar path. A problem is experienced and so a policy is created to fix the problem. Next, the policy is implemented and followed by a period of reflection to see if the problem has been correctly fixed. If it isn't, the process continues until the experience is felt without problems.

If policy is a decision-making process, it calls into question some earlier needs to sustain change. Who's there and who's not? Who has power and who doesn't? Most importantly, who is setting the agenda? And this shows up not just on a grand level at the capital of a state in a closed room. It also shows up when we make decisions about a plan within our organization that will affect many people. Any plan can be a policy. So, in this process, are we being clear (even within a set group) about who's not there, who doesn't have power and who's setting the agenda? Furthermore, are we being clear about the consequences of each one? We need to make sure that we are defining who "we" includes in any group and who it does not. These are crucial questions to reflect on so that true diversity is created. The potential with increased diversity is that it can reduce competition and increase collaboration just by being mindful of who isn't present.

Social justice asks us: what does the change we are seeking mean to people and their livelihoods. How does it genuinely affect people? Public policy, as with all tools in the change agent's toolkit, demands the importance of accurate and intentional goal-setting. When we are striving to include so many varying voices it can seem like a bad idea, for how will any decision ever be made that all will like? It does take time and patience. Consensus-building approaches can aid in removing implementation barriers or moving individuals from one side of a polarity to another. Ultimately, it is about meeting people where they are at, by engaging their participation, listening to them, and finding common values until the two poles are no longer on opposing sides, but rather, standing next to each other.

Public policy is in a state of constant cocreation, so when working with policy we must keep a watchful eye on competition and collaboration. Public policy shows the importance of understanding power, how it shows up, and how it is created. At the base of a power structure is culture and beliefs. These two feed into who gets to be present to create the agenda. From here, the agenda and participants shape the decisions and actions. Public policy, therefore, is a perfect example of using cocreation. It is within the shared purpose and the agenda of an issue where change can start or stop based on who gets to attend. Change agents must remain committed to maintaining the purpose while always asking who isn't present that should be. This was seen with the history of the hunger-relief advocates. In Janet Poppendieck's book, *Sweet Charity*, she talks about hunger-relief advocates and how their role changed over the course of history.[19] During the Great Depression, advocates were advocating for better pay, work relief, and social insurance while intentionally not directly supporting hunger-relief organizations. Originally, advocates saw emergency relief programs as structures that prevented real change from happening. As time went on, these social structures started to be taken apart, piece by piece. The recession of the 1980s left advocates in a rock and hard place.[20] The definition of the problem went from poverty to food because safety nets were being stripped and more weight was being applied to food banks and meal programs. Hunger-relief advocates began changing their agenda. Instead of fighting against these programs, they began to argue for maintaining or increasing funds to emergency food programs. There were many consequences when advocates changed the agenda. One is how we view emergency feeding programs and social safety nets. These programs are no longer emergency only, but provide daily, weekly, and monthly sources of food. Moving from poverty to food also changed legislative priorities among organizations. Instead of work relief and wages that would lift people out of poverty, public policymakers found themselves fighting for the very social safety nets that were never intended to be permanent nor systemic solutions. It changed the agenda, which changed their purpose (from poverty to food) and, from there, changed the public story creating a cascade of consequences. This makes act without acting one of the most important response components within change. Rather than constantly trying to defend with shifting priorities, we can simply maintain the base of the purpose and grow the agenda that will also grow the level of diversity. Act without acting asks us to be with the moment, move with it, and leverage it. For example, when legislators began to strip social safety nets, advocates could have included these legislative matters as a broader definition of antipoverty. Instead of renaming, they could have maintained the name and broadened the definition and story while including more people.

In this story, advocates were originally fighting for antipoverty measures based on a cultural belief that what caused, and could cure, hunger lied within wages, social insurance, and work relief. This created the base of their power structure. This vision was also used to contain who was involved and set priorities whether they meant to or not. Their decisions and actions were guided from here, which also fed to support their cultural beliefs. However, another power structure came into play that had a different set of cultural beliefs and participants. Those stripping the safety nets. Now, their decisions and actions worked to reinforce their cultural beliefs as well. The difference being that since they were the larger power structure, they were able to tell their cultural story to a larger audience. This brought more people into the fold of a hunger story instead of poverty story. In hindsight, the hunger-relief advocates should have maintained their poverty structure in opposition to the hunger structure. At the time of this writing, there are advocates across the country doing just this: redefining the issue back to poverty. Their story illustrates how the immediacy of need can overshadow the need for systemic change. The advocates were put in a very difficult place where a decision had to be made whether to argue for the root causes of hunger, or to argue for the immediate relief of hunger. What matters in this choice is how it changes the definition of the issue. In this case, it moved from poverty to hunger, which changed the legislative agenda for most of these advocates. By changing the definition of the problem, we have modified the cultural understanding of the issue, which might be ultimately hindering the movement.

Public policy is a profound example of how we should all come to the proverbial table when working to create change. Diversity of participants is the first goal. This includes not just individuals, but also groups and organizations. When advocates are beginning their work on an issue such as living wages, they must first create a mind map of all who care or are affected by that issue. When developed, it will surely show many different sectors and groups of people who are connected to it. These are all the people who need to be included whether in meetings or in education. Once here, we need to amplify the different opinions around a living wage. Who's against it and why? Who has concerns and what are they? Who's fiercely for it and why? All this must be developed to create a full picture and attain a shared purpose that all the different groups and sectors can rally behind.

To be able to create this shared purpose, we must look at competition and collaboration by managing the polarities in the room and dropping polarizing language. This will enhance collaboration while reducing competition. However, to fully reduce competition, we must drop our ego that my answer, or my organization's answer, is the end-all right. This can be difficult for people who have been working in the food system for most of their career, but it is of the utmost importance to have cocreation.

Lastly, public policy showcases the differences between the four types of collaboration. Public policy will not work if we are collaborating purely on a transactional level where conversations are not even needed. This is more in the realm of favors or helping someone out because they helped you. There isn't enough trust there. Coordinated collaboration is simply trying to make our schedules line up so that maybe we'll be able to collaborate on our issue. This avenue limits diversity and heightens power for those who can attend. The cooperative model is by far better than the others for policy or change. At least here we are creating coalitions and networks. For something as truly complex as our food system, we need integrative collaboration, which defines cocreation, because in this space we create a shared purpose with high diversity.

Three Approaches to Change

Key to remember in change is that once you feel certain about an answer, you are no longer open to possibilities and differences.

1. Transactional Paradigm
    *   Simple problem-solving techniques. Band-Aids and quick fixes fall here.
    *   Constant state of action and reaction where most of our energy is spent and burnout can happen.
    *   This can be quick change where something is traded for something else.

2. Holistic Paradigm
    *   Whole systems view.
    *   Understanding of paradox. Maybe this is the paradox that to change the food system we need corporations, grassroots organizations, and everything in between in the same room.
    *   Embrace seemingly incompatible ideas and people.
    *   Managing polarity of ideas.

3. Cocreation Paradigm
    *   Building a new system together.
    *   Greatest diversity possible.
    *   Intentional, creative, and diverse dialogues creating new futures and shared visions.
    *   Deep listening and learning from others.

6   Capability Five: Leadership

A complexity view suggests a form of "distributed" leadership that does not lie in a person but rather in an interactive dynamic, within which any particular person will participate as leader or a follower at different times and for different purposes.
— *Lichtenstein, Uhl-Bien and Marion*

Sometimes it seems that leadership positions are more concerned with not only the right answer, but also proving their leadership abilities in a race of ego acknowledgment rather than the right question. Not realizing that the right question will undoubtedly help you get to the answer that is needed for the situation. On the flip side, a typical non-leadership position can sometimes be so concerned with answering "correctly" that one doesn't think about what she should be asking to get at the most relevant answers. Ultimately, what does leadership even mean? *Merriam-Webster* defines a leader as someone who guides or directs an army, movement, or political group.[21] Some synonyms of leader are: chief, commander, director, head, manager, officer, or ruler. It is no wonder that in our culture we only define someone as a leader who has one of those words in her title. If the title lacks the right word, then the individual does not lead. Is this true? Is it possible to be a leader without those words attached to oneself?

Leadership is not "in" a specific position. Leadership can emerge within every interaction. A person, when acting as a leader, is a change agent because when one is acting as leader she must be creating dynamic interactions and disequilibrium so that something new can be created. A leader as change agent nudges the boundaries of comfort and discomfort. She highlights inconsistencies in a way that falls under dynamic conversations. In short, a leader is a facilitator.

Going with the preceding ideas of a leader, we're asked to consider our expert-driven culture. We go to the experts' lectures, we read their books, and, in a manner of speaking, we wait for them to tell us what to do. But, just maybe, we already know what to do. Maybe we all already have some ideas of how we would like to see the food system. Imagine if we realized that we have the power to work together without waiting around for an identified expert or leader. Our expert-driven culture has caused us to lose faith and trust in ourselves and our traditional knowledge. This culture integration starts early with our first days of school going all the way through education where a teacher, an expert, presides over us and tells us what we need to know and how we need to know it. Questions are only to clarify, not challenge, and there is no adding to the lessons. If someone is standing up in front of you talking, then she is the expert and you are not. So be quiet and listen.

In opposition to this style of learning and teaching is something called popular education. It is a methodology that came from the Brazilian educator and writer Paulo Freire, who was writing in the context of literacy and education for poor and politically disempowered people in his country. Popular education asserts that there is no expert and breaks down the wall between teacher and student in which everyone is a teacher and a student. Every individual in a group has something to offer and something to learn. It requires a high degree of participation and uses people's lived experiences and traditional knowledge to learn and to build. We've seen these done as teach-ins during the Occupy movement or through interactive presentations and workshops at organizations and conferences. Even though we call these individuals presenters, they are also teachers. Teaching, or presenting, is a form of leading and, in our culture, being an expert. In some of my activist work, I presented workshops on food justice and food sovereignty. The organization I worked with built presentations that were community driven and drew knowledge from the participants. For example, in many of the presentations the definition of food justice and food sovereignty would be built by the participants. I would only display the technical version toward the end. Activities and group discussion would prevail and by the time we reached those definitions, each would have already been identified and understood. Because I encouraged everyone to find their own voice and to participate, I discovered that although an exact definition of food justice and food sovereignty might still be developing, participants left claiming an understanding of our existing food system. Notably, attendees left with a vision of what they want to see happen with the food system. What is more important: an exact definition or an understanding of how things currently are and where we want to be? We're talking about the difference between theory and practice. Theory provides a foundation while practice provides the walls, hallways, doors, and floors. Practice provides the flow of action.

Capability Five: Leadership

This style of teaching and learning can be challenging because our culture identifies much more to being told what something means and what to do to fix it. Our expert-driven culture looks to others like Michael Pollen to tell us what needs to be done. The only difference between him and anyone else is that he has decided to write extensively about it and make the food system his career. Asking a group to identify issues and visions themselves is difficult at first. I've found, with a little nudging and prompting as a facilitator, that you can direct the conversation into something wonderful where not only do the participants learn, but I also learn from them. An emergent leader exists in this fluid space where at different times we embody a facilitator, a teacher, and a learner. This must be the way through social change so that people feel empowered, diversity is cultivated, decisive moments are created, and actions are amplified. We facilitate so that others have an opportunity to lead. We teach so that others build the confidence to lead. We learn because we are not always leaders.

To maintain certain conditions so that the process of change can be seen through while managing polarities — this is the process of leadership and what is asked of leaders within the system. Usually, you are asked to sit in a space of uncertainty and hold the tension of not knowing. It is significant for change agents to ask what leadership means to oneself. Is it about having the right answers and being able to lead a group of people? Is it about fomenting the answers from the group and providing guidance instead of the path? Or is it something else? Being a leader challenges us to hold multiple perspectives (even ones we may not agree with) and be able to listen to them. Here, we are asked to turn to one another and utilize our differences as leverage instead of walls. The paradox between needing order and chaos all at once will be highlighted in these scenarios. Without chaos, one cannot identify and create change. Having only order gives rise to stagnancy and disease. Chaos lies in disequilibrium and it is the job of the individual as leader to challenge the status quo by creating waves. The transformational challenge requires this to take place.

The first step as a leader is to create disequilibrium in the system based on injustices seen. Disequilibrium can also be created because of gaps that we find between who we say we are and our actual actions. On one level, we have injustices within the food system that need agitation. On another level, we have gaps within our organizing groups and organizations that need agitation. This is where any one individual can give rise to becoming a leader because it can be created by anyone who sees the need for change. At its core, this step deals with surfacing conflict and disrupting patterns. This is not conflict for conflict's sake to simply agitate the system because one can. This is surfacing conflict because of the gaps or injustices we see. Furthermore, conflict will surface naturally here as we call into question our actions. It requires us to disrupt our normal patterns for that is how we provide the spotlight for others to see the same inconsistencies. Here, we can start to see why locating patterns is so integral in change. The patterns that are disrupted are the points of intervention within the system that one has found to leverage. In a traditional environment where leadership is hierarchical, the leader (typically a manager or director) would create an environment where groups are pushed into a new regime disrupting the normal system behavior. In nontraditional environments, a leader may disrupt daily routines via protests or social media like Occupy, Black Lives Matter, or the Coalition of Immokalee

Workers in Florida among many other examples. These groups brought national attention to pertinent issues. Lichtenstein and Plowman, writers on the science of emergent leadership, state that "Dis-equilibrium can be provoked by the pursuit of a new opportunity (e.g. an entrepreneurial project/venture), a threat/crisis from the environment or from within the system, or from fluctuations that alter the entire organizational system."[22] Therefore, disequilibrium means that change agents are placing a spotlight, whatever their methods, on inconsistencies or injustices in the system. This isn't just any spotlight, but one that creates either media, whether social or traditional, or community conversations to show others the gaps you see.

Once here, the condition of amplification begins with new ideas developing, and most importantly, the empowerment of many people to lead. We amplify to create movements whether through conversations or through protests. Amplification happens through the spread of social media, news, rallies, protests, and community conversations. This is a pivotal part of change for leaders. Amplification means broadening the scope and getting more and more people activated. Think of a stone that you toss into water. The ripples created by the stone move outward with the circumference growing larger and larger as the ripples move out. As each ripple broadens, we are engaging with more diverse people and their views. Frenzied and polarized conversations can happen here. During this period, leaders must manage polarities as new ideas are being brought to the table with each new ripple by finding common ground. Change agents can't have judgment in this place about others' views as long as they want to be involved or you think it's important for them to be connected. Creating disequilibrium doesn't stop once we begin amplification, it continues so that the inconsistencies continue to be highlighted and magnified. As the ripples grow wider, we engage and include new community groups, organizations, and individual people into the change movement. The point here is to cast the net as wide as possible, catching as many people as we can.

The third condition that must follow is self-organization. At this point we have identified patterns in the system as well as conflicts and paradoxes. We've also created mass energy around the topic through protests, rallies, social media, community conversations, and the like. The system has become excited and is gaining energy that will continue to grow until its capacity is reached where the system can either collapse or reorganize into something new. Self-organization appears as if it happens completely on its own. However, it requires setting a container that creates the shared purpose where we focus on the differences instead of only the similarities. This is holding space. Secondly, change agents must facilitate transforming dialogues through powerful questions that help people overcome their differences. This requires skilled communication, active listening, and reflection in action. The goal within self-organization is to cocreate the future together through integrative collaboration that reduces competition and increases diversity. Self-organization requires the leaders to be skilled facilitators and communicators. Many of us out there may not consider ourselves skilled in these. That's okay. What's important is to know how crucial these competencies are so that we can continue to learn and grow.

What we want is for the food system to reorganize. In this space, we partner with strange bedfellows and continue to expand our scope of contrasting partners to have an emergence of a new configuration. The last step is stabilizing feedback once we've reorganized. We slow the amplified actions and calm the system down to keep it from spinning out of control. Once we've reorganized, we must stabilize feedback so that we can move forward with our shared vision. This stage happens at the end of change. It's when the change we've been working toward takes effect and becomes the norm. Stabilization doesn't mean that we no longer look at differing viewpoints; it's about maintaining the movement. These steps do not happen in silos. Disequilibrium can still be happening while we are amplifying. Amplifying can still be happening while we are self-organizing.

It is precisely within change that emergence and leadership exist. These occur because of a disruption that can take many forms, such as when structures are thrown into new and diverse interactions or when some sort of gap is shown. These interactions can show up as simple community conversations between seemingly disparate people. Showing a gap refers to a change agent highlighting the gap that exists between a person's perceived reality and actual reality. Emergence shows up as not only ideas and processes, but also in leadership. In Complexity Leadership Theory, it is stated that "A complexity view suggests a form of 'distributed' leadership that does not lie in a person but rather in an interactive dynamic, within which any particular person will participate as leader or a follower at different times and for different purposes."[23] Since change is constant, we must remain adaptive and allow for emergent behavior and patterns from people and the environment. Systems, people, and groups are constantly interacting with each other, are sensitive to changes, and adjust their behavior in the moment in unpredictable ways.

A way of looking at this is with the story of Rosa Parks. What she did was not a random incident that by itself created a cultural shift. It was potentially the tipping point — a juncture of actions amplifying. Rosa Parks had been working with many other change agents who were doing seemingly insignificant actions that together and over time began to move the needle. She and many others were students at the Highlander Folk School, a Tennessee center for training activists for workers' rights and racial equality. These seemingly insignificant acts were strategic actions and protests that were disrupting the normal system, amplifying actions, and creating self-organization around new ideas of being. This is what happens right before new paradigms are formed.

There is an understanding that Rosa Parks was just a random individual who decided to sit in the front of the bus because she could not or was simply too tired to sit in the back. Rosa Parks was giving rise to her decisive moment. She was emerging as a leader. This is important in several ways. First, change happens when people are ready and requires change agents to be constantly nudging the system awake. That is exactly what Rosa Parks and her colleagues were doing. They weren't trying to necessarily force change (and they were at the same time). These activists were highlighting inconsistencies in our culture in hopes that it would wake up other people to it and create a movement, which it did successfully. It was a tipping point.

The second reason that Rosa Parks' story is important is in conjunction with leadership. She was not seen as a leader. She was that random individual doing a random act. This act made her a leader, if nothing else for that moment. This is precisely the leadership that I'm talking about. It is unconventional. It pushes the envelope of our ego because it means that anyone can perform an action that makes her a leader and then move away into the group while someone else steps up to become a leader. A leader is enabling the future as opposed to controlling the future, which simply cannot be done. According to the Tao *Te Ching*, "A knower of the truth does what is called for then stops. He uses his strength but does not force things."[24] This is emergent leadership. It is continually renewing, changing, and shifting who is a leader. The leader is not the "expert" in the room or the speaker at town hall, or the renowned writer, or the director of an organization. To speak correctly, it is all these people and anyone else. Let that sink in for just a moment. Anyone can be a leader or has the potential to lead in a decisive moment. Maybe that leadership role isn't something direct or visual. Maybe it happens through helping others find their voices. And that's what it is: finding one's voice and having the courage to use it.

At the heart of leadership is a constant coming into being and seeing the patterns that are created in that process. This allows us to see intervention points in the system. The food system is also emergent, adaptive, and constantly changing with new ideas, inventions, laws, and environmental challenges requiring emergent leadership. Any system must be built to be adaptive if it is going to be sustainable.

A leader needs to master certain competencies in navigating cultural differences. First is mastering context. The context is the larger environment surrounding and affecting the individual. Leaders can identify and address these larger elements moving from a low-context to a high-context place of being. Insistent pushing toward high-context understanding reduces polarization. When someone doesn't seek to understand the larger picture of what may be going on, but only looks at one specific piece in a particular moment in time, this is low-context. If someone's work begins to decline, for instance, and she is reprimanded and maybe put on an improvement plan without ever being asked if there is anything going on in her personal life, then context is lost as to what may be going on to cause this change. Even more, low-context cultures typically default to the dominant normative due to a lack of context, whereas high-context cultures tend to be multiplistic. High-context is where we look at the whole picture for a better understanding of what is at play. We look beyond just a specific moment in time or singular instance. We look for patterns to see if her work has declined before. We ask the person if there is anything going on that may be affecting her work. We look for a more holistic picture to the person and the situation. Here's an example of how this might play out within a conflict. A situation arises between two people and a third person gets involved to professionally mediate. Within the mediation, the only thing that is discussed is the dispute at hand. Each individual is asked about the specific situation and what person A said and did and what person B said and did — in that moment. The mediator does not ask about cultures and languages or why person B understood person A in a certain way. The mediator does not ask what is going on in each of the individuals' lives outside of the dispute. What happens in a low-context setting is that the dominant paradigm becomes the default normative to define and solve the conflict leaving the non-dominant paradigm out and completely disregarded. In the worst case, the non-dominant paradigm actually hurts the individual's circumstance in the conflict-resolution incident. In a high-context culture, all the above questions and more would be brought to the surface to assess the conflict.

Second, is to know yourself by being aware of your own cultural history and the purviews this has created and shaped. These purviews are our paradigms, beliefs, and truths about the world that are formed by where we were raised, our gender, ethnicity, and class. Understanding our cultural history and how these shape our views, helps us to understand how easy it is for someone else to think differently. Ultimately this broadens our own purviews. Third, is creating a vision for the future. Leaders must manage polarities by taking differing opinions and enlist collaboration and support for unifying these differences into one vision. Furthermore, this form of visioning is not expert or command and control driven. It is driven by diversity, respecting different opinions, and meeting people where they are at so that a shared purpose can be created. Fourth, is about communicating with meaning. Leaders consistently try to find the issues instead of the positions and values instead of the opinions. A leader is trying to connect, not polarize. This comes through in actions more than words. Listening instead of talking, asking questions, and maintaining a desire to understand the person sitting across from you no matter how much you think that you disagree. Lastly, is realizing intention through action. This happens by the leader demonstrating at all times her commitment to bringing people together and transforming conflicts and differences into that shared purpose. It is illustrated through an unwavering sense of patience, compassion, and active listening.

In my own experiences, the feelings of animosity and resentment run rampant among those seeking change. People and corporations on one side are vilified and used as fuel to ignite passion on the other side. These negative feelings are exhausting and aren't sustainable. It takes a lot of energy to continually maintain anger toward someone. Have you ever been angry at a friend or partner? How long are you able to sustain those feelings before feeling exhausted? And who wants to build a movement on hate and resentment? I know when I'm building any sort of relationship those are not the emotions I try to build at the outset. Once those emotions are felt, the relationship is headed south fast.

I'm not saying we can't be angry at certain human and environmental atrocities that take place, or at the lack of government oversight and implementation of regulations, or the defunding of social safety nets, or even at the legislators' will to bend to corporations' fancy. These are reasons to be angry. As leaders, we must direct that anger and channel it. Instead of directing that anger toward people or corporations, keep the anger toward the issue because that is why we are angry. For instance, is anger correctly directed toward Wal-Mart or are we mad at what Wal-Mart is allowed to do? Many workers at Wal-Mart were working toward better wages and treatment in 2013 and still are currently. I briefly worked as an ally with Wal-Mart workers during some of their struggle and learned that none of them wanted to quit their job or vilify Wal-Mart. They simply wanted better treatment and higher wages at their current jobs. They directed their anger toward the issue, not the person or corporation. They supplied evidence of wrongdoing to educate the public and made demands through allied protests, rallies, and strikes. That is a good example of redirecting anger or keeping the anger focused on the issue and not the person. If you think about it, most of what you or I might be angry about is toward the outcomes of events. The events themselves are a confluence, a complex interaction, of parts that need attention with much more than just anger.

As a leader, one would help channel that anger into something sustainable, and ultimately, something with less anger. As was stated earlier, anger can misguide what we should be focused on. We can stay angry about the outcomes that we see happening around us, but we need different emotions for acting. It is pretty much a human given that if someone feels threatened, defenses go up, listening goes down, and plans for actual defense or retaliation take form. It is the animal protectionist in all of us. Using the Wal-Mart example again, if I were to go to a Wal-Mart executive with hate and anger, why should I expect her to return with nothing less than the same? First off, if I'm approaching with hate and anger, I'm not coming to listen. I'm coming to tell her what to do and she better listen to me. Second, if I'm not listening, why should she listen to me? Third, it is simply combative behavior that begets the same type of behavior.

Leaders need to show another way of talking with these entities and to the broader community. A way that shows we're listening and want to hear the other's perspective on what she does and why. This doesn't mean that all along the way we can't be lobbying for better regulations or better enforcement of the regulations already in place. This needs to be done. Someone must take the first step. Why not you? It is time we draw camaraderie from hate.

I close this chapter with the following from Mary-Wynne Ashford: "Sometimes, we look to great individuals like Mother Teresa or Nelson Mandela to see that one person can effect change. I find it more inspiring to see the impact of ordinary people who did what they saw had to be done without becoming great symbols of resistance."[25]

Points to Remember

- Leaders enable the future by highlighting tension, rather than controlling it.
- Small change leads to radical change.
- Nudge disturbances and tensions when they are seen to create emergence.
- Deep leadership begins by defining the problem and asking the right questions.

Complex Adaptive Systems Overview

Lichtenstein and Plowman discuss four main points of CAS and creating change as leaders. The first is creating disequilibrium where conflict is surfaced and we embrace uncertainty and is then followed by amplifying actions by encouraging rich interactions. These do not need to be big events but can be quite simple. One should allow for experiments and support collective action. The third feature is self-organization. This is sense-making as leaders.

After the actions have been amplified, new paths are combined. People naturally self-organize around these new paths. The fourth is stabilizing feedback. After new paths are created and people have self-organized, the system is brought into stabilization. Any system or group cannot stay in that excited state for too long. It becomes stressful and exhausting. Stabilizing feedback is providing normalcy. As a leader, it is your job to facilitate these stages and make sure the group reaches the end, whatever that may be.

7   Capability Six: Systems Thinking

We can't impose our will on a system. We can listen to what the system tells us, and discover how its properties and our values can work together to bring forth something much better than could ever be produced by our will alone.

— Donella H. Meadows

In a systems mind-set, one thinks about the whole system. Individuals take each event as a singular moment in time that is interlaced within a greater framework. Think about a television series. The entirety of all the episodes and seasons compile its whole system. If one episode is watched within the middle of a single season, not much may make sense. It might be funny, dramatic, or entertaining in and of itself, but the larger storyline may get missed. The whole series, from beginning to end, makes up a system. Each episode can be watched independently of others with each episode telling a mini story. But if there is a larger storyline to follow, watching the entire series is the only way to see it.

Another way of looking at it is through a story about a farmer and his son. The farmer and his son owned a horse which ran away. The neighbors exclaimed, "What terrible luck," but the farmer replied, "Maybe or maybe not." When the horse returned leading wild horses with it, the neighbors said, "What luck." But the farmer replied, "Maybe or maybe not." The farmer's son was training one of the new horses and broke his leg. The neighbors all came around saying, "What terrible luck." The farmer replied, once again, "Maybe or maybe not." Later, the military came by requiring all able-bodied men to enlist. Because of the son's injury, he is unable to be enlisted. The neighbors congratulate the farmer for not having his son taken away. The farmer only replied, "Maybe or maybe not." This old Zen story illustrates how we can get caught up in the day-to-day minutiae of our lives and forget to step back and see the whole picture. Only when we step out of our own story, can we see the universal theme or lesson that is inherent in our personal circumstances. In the story, the neighbors and friends of the farmer are only glimpsing the trees within the forest. They do not perceive the forest as a whole. The farmer, on the other hand, is not letting himself get caught up in the details of the trees. He witnesses the trees, but he does not act on each individual happening. He waits for the story to continue. He is looking at the entire storyline uninterrupted. Like the farmer's incidents, each one is a mini story or singular episode being told. His whole life is the greater storyline that is unfolding with each incident. It is self-organizing in that you can't necessarily predict what will happen because each incident either creates new patterns or reinforces preexisting ones.

This is what it takes to have a system perspective. Viewing, or at least recognizing, all the interconnected parts while at the same time refraining from focusing too much on any one piece. By refraining from becoming attached to any one event, we begin to understand that each part is connected to the next like a cause-and-effect dance. This can make an issue very broad as one expands what touches that singular issue. In the television show example, what touches the last show that airs for that series? Every other episode that played before it. Everything builds to that crescendo. Each episode by itself is needed to get to and understand the last show. Each episode can also be watched independently of the others and still be enjoyed though no patterns will be observed. With the farmer story, each incident seen in and of itself appears either positive or negative. When viewed as a whole, the idea of positive/ negative or good/bad becomes blurred.

How does one possess a systems perspective? To be a systems thinker, one needs to practice understanding of how factors influence one another within a whole. Additionally, we need to see, acknowledge, and work with the interconnectedness within a system and maintain an awareness that the whole is greater than the sum of its parts. Part of this thinking is to understand that there are distinct pieces within the system and at the same time these pieces coalesce together to form a whole interlocked in a dance.

Systems thinking asks us to look at the patterns taking shape around an event or issue. Furthermore, it is precisely these patterns that give us insight into the system and where we might intervene to change it. With the television series example, who can identify the patterns of the system? The ones who watched every episode. During the Romantic Movement, Goethe admired "nature's moving order and conceived of form as a pattern of relationships within an organized whole—a conception that is at the forefront of contemporary systems thinking."[26]

What are patterns? A pattern is a unique design like a piece of fabric, something that repeats like a television show that airs each Monday night, or something that always happens in relation to another thing like wanting a drink after a particularly bad day or in celebration of an event. The first two examples show patterns that repeat themselves. The latter example is a pattern of relationships. It is the cause-and-effect dance. An event happens that always triggers an effect, inseparably linking events together like the farmer's son. That is a pattern of relationship because the two events are joined together. Many things in nature, like leaves, have patterns, which are called fractals. These are patterns that continue over and over into infinity. However, many living things tend to have patterns of relationships where the patterns are predominantly in relation to something else either in how they play out, why they happen, or the response to a situation.

If we look at the whole food system, there are a plethora of patterns of relationships that take place continually between the activist to corporation, the activist to change agent, the expert to community member, and so on. There are patterns everywhere in our system that are all based on relationships. Therefore, system thinkers know that we cannot study a system by only looking at the parts sectioned off. Once we disconnect how the parts interact we lose important elements of the system that help us truly understand it, to locate the points of intervention, and to manage the polarities.

This conjures up the phrase: the whole is more than the sum of its parts. When grouped together, the whole is not the sum of its parts. It is something completely new and different. The whole is more than the parts because if each part is conceived of as a pattern of interrelated events and relationships, then that means each pattern is an ingredient partnering with another pattern. Each new organization takes on a pattern that wasn't there before. Already existing patterns interact with new entities generating even more patterns. This continues and is constantly evolving. When viewed as whole, this is the food system. When viewed in parts, it is distribution, policy, farming, hunger relief, institutions, government, and many more. People and organizations are constantly self-organizing and creating new parts within the whole. In these self-organizing systems, the observed phenomena at each level exhibit properties that do not exist at other levels.[27] This means that ideas, patterns, and relationships are emerging every moment at different levels within the system. Life is a good example of emergent properties. We can plan our life all we want, but life events outside of our control always seem to happen and with each event our life becomes altered. A new path is formed with each event or experience making our ability to truly know what will happen in the future impossible. New things are emerging every moment especially if we allow ourselves to see them. Now this can be taken as something terrifying. The world is full of unknowns and possibilities. This can also make it exciting if we stay attuned to it and not hold on too tightly to what we think we know.

An emphasis on the parts of a system is typically referred to as mechanistic or reductionist. System theorists believe that we cannot understand a system by breaking it down into its parts precisely because of the self-organization of relationships that takes place. Breaking it down into parts removes these interrelationships and patterns from being seen and leveraged. It removes the life that makes the system a system to begin with. This ultimately leads to mechanical fixes that rarely resolve root causes because people are operating in silos. These fixes merely provide Band-Aids and at times can even make the scenario worse.

In the book, *The Revolution Will Not Be Funded*, one essay discusses how the rise of nonprofits has created professional jobs out of what used to be known to any person, such as activism or organizing. This also created silos and specialties where individuals work solely on water issues, workers' rights, or agricultural issues. But nary shall these issues, or the people involved, ever meet. The essay maintained that this rise of new professionals is exactly what hinders social justice and movement building. I would have to agree. Silo thinking, or not seeing the forest for the trees, keeps us from seeing the change we wish to see. We must drop this paradigm. They are imaginary and socially constructed, meaning that they can be changed at any time. If a person cares about one specific issue, then she probably cares about a multitude of issues because of how they overlap with one another naturally. Take the issue of food justice. Topics that fall under this include hunger, agriculture, workers' rights, water, soil, fish, animals, indigenous cultures, poverty, wages, and structural racism. This is getting to whole-system thinking and acting. Food, agriculture specifically, is my entry point. It is what brought me into the activist realm and what typically keeps me energized. We all have an entry point that got us involved. This entry point has become, for some of us, our specialty and our silo. Over time, we forget about how we are connected to other issues and may even see other issues in direct opposition to us. For instance, workers and environmental justice activists are pitted against each other because of the feeling that environmentalists remove jobs without thinking about the workers. Then, as more time passes, the separateness becomes normalized and it seems to observers as though there was never a time when things were different. At least until someone asks why, or extends an invitation. This silo isn't just our fault. The essay shows that there has been a movement to create these silos to keep us from creating change. We can break these imagined borders down and begin creating interconnectedness within varying groups by just doing it. Be the courageous individual who finds common ground.

Why is all this important you might be asking. Systems thinking is precisely what a food system change agent needs to do. Applied systems thinking brings it all into the same room and can create powerful partnerships and movements.

The easiest way to see all the interconnections is to create a mind map around food systems. It could look something like this:

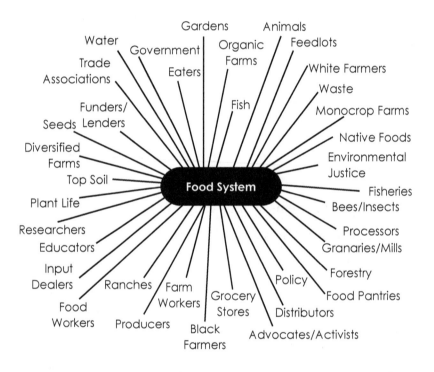

This is just an example. There is even more that could be added to this illustration. However, this graphic illustrates how many people, organizations, and companies are affected by food. This is a view into the whole system and a visual example of how the whole is more than the sum of its parts. Each of these parts is a self-organizing structure that carries many patterns. When seen as a whole, we see a highly interconnected web that is constantly changing and reorganizing with each new collaboration. We can see it as either a hopelessly complicated endeavor where it is impossible to truly include the whole system or as a wealth of possibilities, an ongoing chain of partnerships. What if this was genuinely tapped into? What if input dealers and farm workers or environmental justice and seed companies sat in a room together? Who knows the types of conversations that could be had in that space if facilitated well? There could be a movement like no other. The trick is finding those common values. It is with common values that the overlaps between the varying groups start to become apparent. The circumvention is looking beyond why groups may not work together and look squarely at why we do what we do and how that overlaps with others.

Systems view looks beyond hierarchical structures and views the whole as a web. In the networks mentioned above, it might be rather easy to imply that some are more important than others for whatever reasons. This is a human problem that we seem to do everywhere. Apply some sort of hierarchical structure creating greater-than and less-than sectors. We do this even when we strive to have horizontal organizations and leadership. It happens so naturally we must stay mindful always to maintain a nonhierarchical structure much like a loving relationship needs constant nurture and attention. Fritjof Capra sums this up nicely: "…the web of life consists of networks within networks. At each scale, under closer scrutiny, the nodes of the network reveal themselves as smaller networks. We tend to arrange these systems, all nesting within larger systems, in a hierarchical scheme by placing the larger systems above the smaller ones in a pyramid fashion. But this is a human projection. In nature, there is no 'above' or 'below,' and there are no hierarchies. There are only networks nesting within other networks."[28]

Let's go back to the visual showing the interconnected networks surrounding a food system. You are asked to view them as interconnected and nested networks where each has emergent properties when interacting with another network creating new networks at each meeting point. To leverage all these networks would be powerful and creative, and could create a tipping point of change. If we look at each network's function instead of its specifics, we are once again getting to that common ground. It is here, within common ground, that we find alliances.

Another way to look at systems theory is through permaculture. Permaculture is a way of growing food that looks at the whole system and has each plant and environmental component working together to maximize effectiveness. Permaculture looks at and identifies the world in layers and guilds. Much like the systems description above with complex layers or networks building upon each other, permaculture looks at layers to understand how the plant, animal, and insect world interact together. Each layer is a complex network that interacts with the layers above and below it. For example, one layer would be the soil and the microbes and roots, the next would be the ground cover, animals, and insects, next would be a layer that sits atop the previous, and so on. In a human-constructed world of permaculture, we create guilds. A guild is usually defined as an association of people working toward a common goal. In permaculture, a guild is a grouping of plants, animals, insects, and other natural components that also work together to help ensure their survival. Instead of planting gardens, permaculture teaches us how to "build guilds." Instead of teaching about specific plants, we teach about the plant's functions or how it interacts with its surroundings. Similarly, within food justice, we can group not by our visual similarities, but by how we interact together. Within interplanting techniques, one is advised to either plant shallow with deep-rooted vegetables or short with long season. Opposites. Nature soars in the world of diversity and we are a part of nature. What if we followed these techniques? Just think of the amazingly creative and lively partnerships that could be sparked with this kind of action.

In creating our interconnectedness, we must become flexible to the results we envision. Everyone has a slightly different result they may want to see. If you read food justice books, you probably know that there are visions of a new food system being drawn up all the time. But these visions are not collectively created, but are collectively disseminated. In my group work, I relinquish any desire toward a specific result. More specifically, I create my own groundlessness and potential insecurity because I believe in the rightness of the process. I put the weight on the process because I know if it is well thought out and well facilitated, the results will be exactly what they need to be. This happens because there is a form of integrative collaboration taking place, there is high inclusion, and silo thinking is being bridged among different groups. In these group processes, we access the shared values among the team and move forward from that space.

Systems thinking is most practiced when we are strategically planning. Formal strategic thinking has had two paths in deciphering a strategic plan. The first path is more formal than not and includes looking at tangible weaknesses and strengths. Think of the SWOT analysis with strengths, weaknesses, opportunities, and threats. This process is very concrete, providing a limited capability of only coming up with what you know. There is another path that creates a space where creativity can take place for what could happen, whether positive or negative. To begin this process, we may need to start with some creative strategizing. I use "begin" loosely here. Individuals working in the food system have been in the process of strategizing for a long time if for no other reason than it is an ongoing process. Strategic planning can be used as change models. New change agents replace previous generations. There have been men and women fighting for food safety, better regulations, more locally based food, and for a sustainable system since the industrial food system began. This makes looking at strategies and change models for long-term activism even more important.

To do this, we need to broaden our scope and open ourselves to what might seem impossible or even absurd. For starters, instead of calling it strategic planning, which makes us all think more of plans than actions, let's call the process a change model. If we are going to diagnose the food system, for example, we would start with naming the current environment. Everything and anything that comes to your mind falls into this segment. There is no wrong answer. We could say that there is a rise of conservatism, people are spending less, the economy still isn't picking up, structural racism within the food system, people struggle to find employment, loss of cultural food ways, social safety nets are being removed, and so on. What one sees in the environment doesn't have to be a direct or indirect connection to the food system. Even though it inherently will, since the food system is connected to just about everything.

Capability Six: Systems Thinking

This is where it starts to get fun and imaginative. The environmental scan is extrapolated to create probable and desired futures. A probable future is one in which we believe it will most likely happen. A desired future is one in which we want it to happen disregarding whether we believe it can take place. From here, current realities are decoded and translated. This is as concrete and realistic as one can get with what is currently happening within the food system — good and bad. Two sets of strategies are fashioned to adapt to probable futures and those influence our desired futures. This is an important step. Paths are created to deal with a future we may not entirely like, while at the same time building plans to get closer to where we ideally want to be. This is much like the hunger-relief advocates who shifted strategies to changing circumstances. However, the piece that seemed to be left out was the strategy and plan to continue pushing for their original desired future. Equal weight needs to be given to both. Next, goals are created from these strategies with each one having an enabler and disabler identified. An enabler is something that helps the goal, and a disabler is something that will hinder the goal. Lastly, an action plan for moving forward is created based on the goals, enablers, and disablers. I've used this model for cross-departmental work where many felt they were never listened to or even included in program changes. When I facilitated this, it meant that I didn't get to directly participate in the process, which might concern some. However, I knew if I had enough diversity and inclusion in the room, the plan that was created would be appropriate. The result was something that everyone was excited about to see take shape over the next five years. Even though this example is an internal organization one, there are many other times I've used the same structure for community workshops to clarify purpose and build an action plan.

I began by thinking who needed to be there. I invited ten to fifteen staff members from every department within the agency who touched the program in various ways such as funding, deliveries, ordering, planning, purchasing, and warehousing. I led us through the process of the environmental scan, and then we talked about what probable futures we saw for the program. After this, I asked people to think about what desired futures they could envision for the program. This step can be difficult as people tend to get stuck on realities. I took time and gave some examples of what this could look like, where one of my examples was completely changing the format of the current program. Once we got going, people couldn't stop thinking of other potentials for the program of what we could do. Then we looked at our current realities, which took the shape of what we were lacking and not lacking. Then we looked at adaptive and influencing strategies that would help us get closer to our probable and desired futures. We came up with a lot of strategies. Finally, from these strategies we identified our top five goals for the program. I laid complete trust in the process and walked into it saying to myself that whatever came out of it is what needs to be. My supervisor was very nervous about the process afterward. She asked if what we ended up with is what I wanted. It absolutely was because it was built by the group. It was a unified vision and action plan where everyone felt that their voices were heard. I knew that I would be on board with whatever came of it, because it was decided by all the people involved in the program. All my facilitation is led in predominantly the same way. I don't go in hoping for certain outcomes. I go in with the certainty that my process will bring about whatever needs to happen. My hope is tied to the process, not the outcome. Vaclav Havel, a Czech writer, philosopher, dissident, and statesman, said, "Hope is not the conviction that something will turn out well, but the certainty that something makes sense regardless of how it turns out."[29] This is absolutely true of change.

Systems thinking, permaculture, and integrative collaboration all have one thing in common. Each is a concept for understanding the big picture and provides implementation techniques to help understand and work it. These concepts help us see the whole system, as well as find ways to make it seem possible to have the whole system in the room. They let us know that the impossible can happen and that it will take some time. Joanna Macy wrote as follows: "Since you cannot see into the future, you simply proceed to put one stone on top of another, and another on top of that. If the stones get knocked down, you begin again, because if you don't nothing will get built."[30] We must stay the course and viewing the room with a whole systems perspective will not only help us get there, but it will help us maintain hope even when there may not be any reason for optimism.

Notes on Systems Thinking

- When all is in chaos that is the time to create anew. A whole systems solution must be effective to the entire system, not just one piece.
- If you want to shift a paradigm, look at it like a metaphor. Take two unrelated views and create a metaphor out of it to stretch your brain to think where the commonalities might exist. This metaphor creates a paradox that can be the catalyst for dialogue on change. It's about the question, not the answer. For instance, try unpacking: access to farms reduces access to food or nonaction is action. The paradox requires a paradigm shift.
- The harder you push, the harder the system pushes back.
- Small changes can produce big results, but the areas of highest leverage are often the least obvious.
- There is no blame. The cure lies in your relationship with the opponent.
- Reactive and proactive actions are guided by past experiences and patterns. While innovation happens in the present moment because of that particular moment.
- Within systems, leaders must manage instead of attempting to solve problems.

8   A New Direction

Do not depend on the hope of results…you may have to face the fact that your work will be apparently worthless and even achieve no results at all, if not perhaps opposite to what you expect. As you get used to this idea, you start more and more to concentrate not on the results, but on the value, the rightness, the truth of the work itself…In the end it is the reality of personal relationship that saves everything.

— *Thomas Merton*

Our food system has changed immensely over the last two hundred years. It doesn't look anything like it once was because it is a system that is constantly emerging. It's full of people who are trying to make it better than what it is or was. We may not agree with what some of these people have pushed forward. However, at one time and in some form, most of these were developed to make the system more efficient and productive. This in turn was to make the farmers' and workers' lives easier and increase food for us all to those who pushed for it. For lack of a better phrase, these things were invented to help us in some form. It was someone's idea on how the food system could be improved based on what the scenarios were at that time. We don't have to agree with them.

But I think we can all agree that no one invented these things with the core desire to hurt people even if these become the consequences. Some were to intentionally make things easier or better. Some were invented to increase profit sharing and organizational growth.

Many times, people have felt that the core goal was profit-making. Getting food to people was merely a secondary concern. A dive into our food history shows agribusiness, political, and economic groups working together to make food-product ingredients cheaper for themselves so that profits increase; ever more consolidation to once again increase profit sharing; and removing price supports for farmers providing opportunity for agribusiness to squeeze additional profits.

For our growers, food is a business. The business of growing and selling food to processors, grocers, or directly to consumers. Farmers are hugely diverse and come from many different cultural backgrounds. Growers are lovers of land, farming, and owning their own business. Some farmers suffer from great happiness and success, while others suffer from a constant struggle for survival striving not to lose their business and their family farm. Some farmers feel trapped, yet some feel free. Other farmers are gripped with the reality of what farming has become and the deafening history of American farming as they watch another farmer fall to the wayside. Growers' profits are squeezed by processors, distributors, seed companies, and other input-agribusiness companies. Furthermore, as food corporations continue to consolidate across the entire food chain, farmers are forced to get big or get out. Growers leave the land and move to urban counterparts because farming isn't viable.

Eaters pay increasing amounts for specialty foods like organic, gluten-free or all-natural, while processed and fast foods keep getting cheaper. Large corporations that supply some of these foods are held suspect as to whether they are providing these foods for their value or the potential price tag that can be correlated with it. We have also jumped leaps and bounds with industrialization and modernization as our cities grow. This has largely left out our rural counterparts with food being either too expensive or hard to reach without proper transportation.

Food touches everything. It might be one of the largest
systems because of its web-like connectors to every other field
and system. Food is connected to humans, insects, animals,
plants, climate, loggers, fishers, farmers, eaters, tribal groups,
transportation, distribution, retail, politics, economics, culture,
health care, advertising, law, banking, mining, construction,
defense, education, processing, water, soil, foundations,
nonprofits, tourism, lobbyists, railroads, religion, arts,
entertainment, and many more. Additionally, our food history
is steeped in colonialism, slavery, and racism. Food has a far
reach with each sector having some advocate for its field that
is either directly or indirectly affecting the food system. This
creates inherent conflict and difficulty with the work ahead.
Deeply entrenched issues around racism, colonization, and
gender equality require attention to how we hold space,
communicate, and manage diverse opinions while we try to be
as inclusive as possible. Rough conversations lie before us and
challenge each of us to learn from one another while also
suspending judgments and assumptions.

Mainly because of the industrial push, the food system has
had challenging moments of intense growing pains. There

have been food-safety horror stories in the late 1800s, to a puritanical view toward food in the early 1900s, and finally to a desire for affordable year-round food that consumers have grown so accustomed to. The former two directly link to the rise of industrial food and the fear it instilled in people as industrialized food was burgeoning. The latter is linked to the industrial system because it helps drive it. Year-round food requires processing, trade, and industrialization. While at the same time of all this, corporations have been increasingly trying to figure out how to boost their profit margins.

The industrialization of the food system was helped by advertising. Media has been used throughout history to help change the cultural normative. For instance, food safety from the early 1900s was smoothed over with the aid of magazines. Agribusiness and organizations would partner with well-known voices that were used to sell meat that traveled far distances or all-in-one baking mixes. In both examples, advertising was used to help soothe the public so that they would purchase, or continue to purchase, the product. To make it more complicated, one of the reasons for finding ways to ship meat and other products for long distances was because of the growing urban areas. More food was needed in larger areas that did not support, or offer, places to grow your own food. Alternatives had to be found, even while people still felt that food should be produced as close as possible to where one lived. Media played a pivotal role in helping to sell products that weren't local as the urban areas were expanding by leaps and bounds.

There is something quietly being said within these words. This book has given much precedence to working with individuals of opposing sides by focusing on the issue rather than who one is. You have been consistently asked to look beyond so you can listen to what is being said and act within the moment instead of actions based on the past. We can begin to understand the importance of this as we look at the history and state of our food system.

We must ask ourselves what it is that we want to sustain. When we think about the meaning of words, sustain means to maintain something, to keep doing the same thing so that it is sustainable. However, *sustainability* is an emerging process where an idealized and fixed state does not exist much like our food system. We need to shift to be sustainable over time because *sustainability* is something that is constantly changing. It is a process of becoming and cannot be attached to a certain fixed vision. This also means that to a certain degree the path is completely unknown.

How can something be unknown if we have a plan and vision as to what we want? Just as in our own lives, whether professional or personal, we may have a specific outcome that we want for ourselves, yet we usually find ourselves quite surprised how we got there. Not only that, the *there* can look different than how we imagined. This is the type of emergence that change agents must submerse themselves in. We can have tenets for the change we seek within the food system, or any system for that matter, and we also need to be open to how we get there and what those tenets look like in real life.

The capabilities reviewed here are simplistic and maybe even obvious. When practiced intentionally out in the community, the process will be difficult. Deeply entrenched issues of racism, colonization, and gender inequities will rise up within many conversations that we will all have to face. These tough conversations will necessitate each of us to socially reconstruct on some level as our assumptions and judgments are tested and questioned. We should allow for them to be tested, as well as allow ourselves to test those in others. This is why the six capabilities are so important. Each of these is required to effectively create highly integrated sustainable change. We are going to find ourselves in highly charged conversations that, if we want to make any headway, we will have to think about the space we create, how we communicate within that space, who we did not invite and why. We will need to be able to reflect in the moment as we may be hearing things that create conflict within ourselves or others. We will need to be actively listening in these conversations so that we can be intentional, and not defensive, with our responses. It is okay to hold on to our own beliefs and suspend them for a brief moment so that we may hear what the other person is saying. Not only hear them, but inquire into their opinions in an honest, nonthreatening way. We all will experience a moment within these capabilities and conversations where we will have something to learn, to let go of, or suspend.

It is tantamount within this framework that we recognize our lens and the power we have or don't have and how this affects our actions. Some segments are religion, sexual orientation, race, level of education, age, class, and able-bodyism. This is critical to look at within oneself to see how your lens shapes your view of the world. Just as important is for this to provide insight into why others might view the world the way that they do. The other essential piece of this is to understand that many people do not get to choose where they fit into the power structure. It has been chosen for them. If I don't recognize my lens, then I can't hold space or communicate to the best of my ability, which leads to me being unable to cocreate with a diverse group, lead or view the entire system. I will not see my assumptions within the system that could be holding me back from integrated collaboration. Identifying my lenses doesn't mean I will, or even can, shed them off and identify with other groups. It is simply understanding myself more deeply so that I can create change more effectively.

Integrated collaboration doesn't mean a molding of thoughts where we all need to view the world the same by giving up our own desired futures. We're not trying to create sameness, a mass group of cookie cutters. The work laid out here is creating something wholly new that within it contains all our varying lenses and with a shared purpose of all our desired futures. To be clear, this shared purpose cannot contain racism, sexism, heterosexism, classism, able-bodyism, or ageism. At the same time, those who may be guilty of these views must be included in our work. They can't be left out just because of what they say or how they feel about some people, for the main reason that we will not be creating real, sustainable change if we leave them at the sidelines. The kind of change I talk about here makes it imperative that everyone is included, which is why finding common values are so important. In some circumstances, this is going to feel impossible, which is why we must constantly practice and hone our skills within the capabilities of engagement.

This can create a lot of anxiety in ourselves and others that we'll have to learn to deal with. For these moments, I like the definition that Margaret Wheatley gave the word "hopelessness."[31] She says that hopelessness is about being without hope. Hope connotes dreaming or longing for something. Hope suggests expectations. When these hopes, expectations, or dreams do not come into fruition, we are let down. We feel as if we failed because it didn't happen exactly as we had hoped. Heard that phrase before? "It didn't go as I'd hoped." However, what Wheatley is offering to us in the word "hopelessness" is the ability to let go of that dream or expectation. To reside in a space where we do not hope for things, but instead keep working on issues that align with our values and removes the need for hope. Hope arises out of holding dearly to a specific vision and out of wanting to pretend as if we can singularly control what happens in the future. Creatively using and responding to change asks us to reside in this space of hopelessness, in this space of nonattachment. We must give in to the fact that we don't know what is going to happen next. We don't know what kinds of consequences will spiral out from our actions. And despite our best planning we can't ever see all the forces at play. Any one person who decides to reflect in action changes the path from that point, which in turn can change many other paths giving rise to a multitude of possible outcomes. We must find this hopelessness.

This is not to be taken negatively. Hopelessness breaks us from these chains and allows us to see possibilities in every minute of life and grab a hold of it, if we choose to see. Hopelessness is letting go of our preconceived future and stepping into the present moment. There is another term other than "hopelessness" from a poet named John Keats. It's called negative capability; that is, "when a man is capable of being in uncertainties, mysteries, doubts, without any irritable reaching after fact and reason."[32] It is to realize that we can never truly know or say how the world works and that it is ever-changing. It is difficult to remain in this space and is freeing. It's freeing because it pushes us to be in the present moment, allows for us to have uncertainties, and to be able to hold others' truths, no matter how different, without hate or judgment.

Creatively using and responding to change asks a lot of us. We all have expectations. We also have ideas of people and groups based on past encounters or stories. However, we must let go of the past and the future if we are to truly embrace a new direction. For, if we let go of past and future and work with all the groups we need to change the food system—friend or foe—then we are absolutely embracing change and sustainability. Remember, whatever wants to happen is what needs to happen in that moment.

What I'm getting ready to say may not be what most people want to hear, let alone think about. I know that I may not see the change that I want to see in my lifetime. Sometimes change takes a very long time and we never know when that tipping point will arrive showing the light at the end of the tunnel. Even more, we don't even know what that point will look like even though we have all these predefined visions. It is a known unknown whether we want to admit it or not. So, it's important as change agents that we find the means to keep us inspired so that we don't give up. What ignites you in your issues? I look at the core values underneath what I'm doing for those are what keep me going in whatever work I find myself in. Those core values override any exhaustion that I may feel. They also help to find my path when I've gone astray. In this, I'm able to relax into intentions, values, and gradual change. Pessimism lifts because who knows what the next iteration of the food system will look like. All we can do here and now is shine a light on what is just and unjust and remain inquisitive of those with different views with a core of kindness and honest curiosity.

Unpredictable conditions are all around us as humans. Our food system is constantly growing in complexity, shifting and hardening in culture. The more we control how food is grown, the more it can't survive without constant inputs. The more we control anything, the more it requires us to be ever vigilant over its actions because it's in the others' nature to push against the control. Control comes from many places: fear, anger, or being set within a certain vision. Control needs to be relinquished by dealing with our fears and anger. Ask ourselves why those feelings exist so that they can be cast aside. As for being set within a certain vision, let go of the hope, controlled notions, and future expectations around that vision so that others can build into it with their own. We can be in the present moment without any inclination to control for future endeavors. We can remain in uncertainties, mysteries, and doubts without madly scraping for clarity or a singular clear direction.

How do we successfully capture and sustain this space? We must remember to separate people from issues and define the issue as clearly as possible. This will help us find common values. From here, we can then locate an effective point of intervention by finding and assessing the patterns. Remember, we are not resolving different viewpoints, but managing them. Therefore, we must learn polarity management because we want different viewpoints in the same room. Here, let go of your ego and the need to be right.

Within this space be a teacher, a facilitator, and a learner.

Lastly, immerse yourself in the six capabilities of engagement.

Notes

Chapter 1
Engaging in Change

1. *The Revolutionary,* Dirs. Irv Drasnin, Lucy Ostrander, and Don Sellers; Perf. Sidney Rittenberg, 2012.
2. Robert Heilbroner, *The Worldly Philosophers* (New York: Touchstone Publishing, 1999).
3. Julie Battilana and Tiziana Casciaro, "The Network Secrets of Great Change Agents," *Harvard Business Review*, July–August 2013, 62-68.
4. John Dewey, *Democracy and Education* (Teddington, Middlesex, UK: Echo Press, 2007).

Chapter 2
Capability One: Holding Space

5. S. A. McLeod, "Social Identity Theory," 2008, Retrieved from www.simplypsychology.org/social-identity-theory.html.
6. Joan V. Gallos, *Organization Development* (San Francisco: Jossey-Bass, 2006).
7. The Cross Cultural Health Care Program, Retrieved from http://xculture.org/cultural-competency-programs/about-cultural-competency/
8. Margaret Wheatley, *Finding Our Way* (San Francisco: Berret-Koehler Publishers, 2005).

Chapter 3
Capability Two: Communication

9. Edwin E. Olson and Glenda H. Eoyang. *Facilitating Organization Change* (San Francisco: Jossey-Bass/Pfeiffer, 2001).

10. Barry Johnson, *Polarity Management* (Amherst, MA: HRD Press, 1996).
11. Kenwyn K. Smith and David N. Berg, *Paradoxes of Group Life* (San Francisco: Jossey-Bass, 1987), 3.
12. John Heider, *Tao of Leadership* (Palm Beach, FL: Green Dragon Publishing, 2015), 57.
13. Kenneth Cloke and Joan Goldsmith, *Resolving Conflicts at Work* (San Francisco: Jossey-Bass, 2011).

Chapter 4
Capability Three: Reflection in Action

14. Donald Schön, *Educating the Reflective Practitioner* (San Francisco: Jossey-Bass, 1987).
15. Paul Loeb, *The Impossible Will Take Little Awhile* (New York: Basic Books, 2004).
16. Donella Meadows, *Thinking in Systems* (White River Junction, VT: Chelsea Green Publishing, 2008).
17. Loeb, *The Impossible Will Take Little Awhile*, 349.
18. Donald Schön, *Educating the Reflective Practitioner*, 68.

Chapter 5
Capability Four: Cocreation

19. Janet Poppendieck, *Sweet Charity?* (New York: Penguin Group, 1998).
20. Leslie Mikkelsen, *Sweet Charity?*, March 2014, http://www.eatbettermovemore.org/charity.html.

Chapter 6
Capability Five: Leadership

21. "Leader." Merriam-Webster.com. Merriam-Webster, n.d. Web. 16 Aug. 2016.
22. Benyamin B. Lichtenstein and Donde Ashmos Plowman, "The Leadership of Emergence," *The Leadership Quarterly* 20:4 (August 2009): 617–30.
23. Benyamin B. Lichtenstein et al., "Complexity Leadership Theory," *Emergence: Complexity & Organization* 8:4 (November 2006): 2–12.
24. Lao Tzu and Jonathan Star, *Tao Te Ching* (New York: Penguin Group, 2001), 38.
25. Paul, *The Impossible Will Take Little Awhile*, 332.

Chapter 7
Capability Six: Systems Thinking

26. Fritjof Capra, *The Web of Life* (New York: Doubleday, 1997), 21.
27. Ibid., 28.
28. Ibid., 35.
29. Paul, *The Impossible Will Take Little Awhile*, 349.
30. Ibid., 329.

Chapter 8
A New Direction

31. Margaret Wheatley, *So Far from Home* (San Francisco: Berret-Koehler Publishers, 2012.
32. John Keats, *Selections from Keats's Letters*, October 2009, Retrieved from http://www.poetryfoundation.org/learning/essay/237836?page=2.